Working on Words

Working on Words

John F. Canney   J. Philip Goldberg   Diane D. O'Connor

Gallaudet College Press   Washington, D.C.

Published by the Gallaudet College Press
Kendall Green, Washington, D.C. 20002

Gallaudet College is an equal opportunity employer/educational institution. Programs and
services offered by Gallaudet College receive substantial financial support from the U.S.
Department of Education.

ISBN 0-913580-72-4

contents

a word to the teacher

Working on Words is a series of vocabulary lessons for intermediate and advanced students of English as a second language. These lessons, or units, seek to develop both a receptive and expressive command of words frequently used in everyday life. All of these words are rather abstract so that meaning cannot easily be communicated by reference to pictures or concrete objects but must be conveyed in words. The definitions in this text depart markedly from classical definition in form. This departure was deliberate and reflects our attempt to make the essential meaning of abstract terms as immediately accessible as possible to the students. We have also taken great pains to phrase all explanatory material and exercises in terms that are within the receptive grasp of intermediate students of English. Each definition is followed by one or more sentences which illustrate how the word may be used.

Many students may already know some of these words receptively, though they still need extensive writing practice before they can use them expressively. For this reason, the students quickly move from initial receptive exercises to a series of controlled expressive exercises and, finally, to a free writing assignment of a story or paragraph at the end of each unit.

For every five units we include a pretest, a review, and a post test. Each unit teaches 10 words, all chosen for inclusion in the unit because of their close relationship to the other words in the unit. Thus, all of the words taught in a unit could naturally occur together in a real communicative situation. In addition, each unit presents a number of so-called "related words," or words derived from the new words taught.

Blank spaces frequently occur in a list of "related words." This means either that no word exists in that part of speech category or that we have chosen not to teach the word that does exist in that category.

Although the exercises provide both receptive and expressive practice, *Working on Words* is not a grammar and structure text. Our brief introductory unit, entitled "Parts of Speech," is intended to provide students with the minimum grammatical knowledge necessary to make correct receptive choices between lexically similar items. To help students use the new words expressively, we have included in "grammar boxes" structural patterns necessary to form grammatical sentences. But apart from this, the teacher will find that in their expressive exercises students reveal all of the grammar and structure problems they might normally be expected to show in their free writing. We are fully aware of this problem but leave its solution to the teacher. Most teachers will probably wish to correct grammar and structure only in relation to the information in the "grammar boxes." Some may wish to correct all errors in grammar and structure.

This book has been designed to allow great flexibility in its use. It is suitable for either individualized instruction or a classroom-centered approach. The Answer Key in the back allows for the self-correction of objective exercises, if desired, while free writing exercises require correction by the teacher. The perforated pages allow even more flexibility. Some teachers may want to collect exercises as each student finishes a lesson. Others will prefer to correct exercises in the classroom and keep the books intact. Some teachers may wish to collect all pretests and post tests to use them for grading purposes. Teachers will be able to decide for themselves how best to use this book after becoming familiar with the plan of each unit as outlined in the "Introduction."

John F. Canney
J. Philip Goldberg
Diane D. O'Connor

Gallaudet College
Kendall Green
Washington, D.C.

introduction

Working on Words is a new way of learning vocabulary. Some of the words you see in the units in this workbook may seem easy for you. Others may be harder. Your goal is to learn the meaning of each word. Your goal is also to learn how to use these words in your own sentences. Each section of every unit will help your vocabulary grow. There are 10 new words in each unit, but you will learn many related words, too. You will also learn how prefixes and suffixes and word-roots help to build your vocabulary.

A WORD ABOUT THE UNITS

Study the following information about the units in *Working on Words.* Every unit is organized in the same way.

Definitions and Examples

In the first section of each unit you will find:

• The new words to learn.

• The part of speech of each new word to learn. It is important for you to know whether a word is a noun (n), a verb (v), an adjective (adj), or an adverb (adv). It is also important to remember that **n** means noun, **v** means verb, **adj** means adjective, and **adv** means adverb. If you have any questions about the parts of speech, study "Parts of Speech" beginning on page 10.

• A short definition of each new word to learn. These units do not teach every meaning of a word. They teach only the most useful meanings.

• Each new word in a sentence. The sentences will help to make the meanings clearer.

• An asterisk (*) next to some words. You will see a box with information about any word with an asterisk. This box is very important. It means that there is something special about the word—a pattern you need to know or something about its meaning. This is an example:

---

*To use this word correctly, you need to know this pattern.

      want + noun

      want + to + verb

Example: I want a **dog.**
          I want **to play** baseball.

Want cannot be followed by **verb** + **-ing.** We *cannot* say:

    ~~I want playing baseball.~~

You might understand the meaning of a word but still make a mistake in using it. The information in the boxes will help you use the words correctly in your own sentences.

• Blanks to fill in with new words. You will complete sentences with words from the unit. Sometimes more than one word will fit into a blank. Do not worry about that. Just fill in each blank so that you have a correct English sentence.

Word-Roots, Word-Beginnings (Prefixes), and Word-Endings (Suffixes)

The second section of each unit will show you how the parts of a word go together and how they work. Learning how a prefix or suffix works in one word will help you understand how it works in other words.

This section also lists related words. Related words are words which go together. They include new words and words made by adding suffixes or prefixes to the new words. You should try to use some of these words in your writing. We list related words in this order: verb, noun, adjective, adverb. Sometimes you will see a blank in a list of related words. This blank means that the unit does not teach you a related word for that part of speech. Do not try to use a key word or a related word as that part of speech. For example:

sadden (v)
sadness (n)   happiness (n)
sad (adj)   happy (adj)
sadly (adv)

This means that the unit does not teach a verb or an adverb for *happy*. Do *not* write:

~~I happy.~~

or

~~I happy you.~~

or

~~He helped me happy.~~

Using These Words

There are three kinds of exercises in the third section of each unit.

In the first exercise you pick the correct word for a sentence from two words in parentheses. First, decide what kind of word goes in that place in the sentence—noun, verb, adjective, or adverb. Knowing the kind of word may help you with the answer. If you still do not know the answer, you must decide which word fits the meaning of the sentence. Sometimes you must choose between two words which are the same part of speech. The words may have almost the same meaning but use different patterns in grammar. For example, you might have the sentence:

I (enjoy/like) to play baseball.

In this sentence you would choose **like** because **enjoy** cannot be followed by **to + verb.**

The second kind of exercise begins with one or more short paragraphs for you to read. Next, there are some sentences which show how to use words in the unit to talk about the paragraph. The sentences will be examples for you when you write your own sentences.

Next, you will read a story. You will then write three or four sentences of your own about the story, using some of the new words you learned. For example:

You read: John was thinking about what he did yesterday.
He went to the park. He ate his lunch there with his friends.

You write: John **recalled** what he did yesterday.
John **remembered** what he did yesterday.
John **enjoyed** his visit to the park.

In the third kind of exercise you will write a paragraph of your own. Use five or more of the new words or related words from the unit you are studying in your paragraph.

After you complete a unit, try to use the new words as often as you can in your own writing.

A WORD ABOUT REVIEWS AND TESTS

For every five units of *Working on Words* you will find a pretest, a review, and a post test.

Pretest

A pretest is a very short test to find out if you need to do the five units. Each pretest has two parts:

• Receptive—matching the words in the units with their synonyms.

• Expressive—writing sentences using the words in the units.

Your mistakes will show which units you need to do.

Review

The review gives more practice with the words you studied. Some teachers will give the review after you finish the five units. Other teachers will give you the review after the post test, if you need it. Your teacher may not ask you to do the review at all. Or you might do it much later to see how much you remember.

Post Test

Each post test contains six exercises:

• Synonyms. You will match words with words which mean the same or nearly the same.

• Antonyms. You will match words which mean the opposite or nearly the opposite.

• Prefixes, Suffixes, and Roots. You will identify the part of speech of each word using the suffixes you studied. Or you might use prefixes you studied to make new words.

• Multiple Choice. You will pick the correct word to complete a sentence.

• Sentence Formation. You will write your own sentences using words from the units you studied.

• Paragraph Writing. You will write two short paragraphs (about five sentences each) using words you studied.

You should try to score 90% or above on the tests.

ROOTS, PREFIXES, AND SUFFIXES

Word-Roots, Word-Beginnings (Prefixes), and Word-Endings (Suffixes)

A word-root is the basic part of a word. For example, **write** is a word-root. You know that it is also a word. In English, some roots can stand alone as words. Some roots cannot stand alone. We must add something to them to make them words. We add word-beginnings (prefixes) or word-endings (suffixes) to word-roots. If you add to the front of a root, you add a prefix. If you add to the end of a root, you add a suffix. Prefixes and suffixes are ways of building new words and making new meanings from word-roots.

Prefixes and suffixes are never used alone, but they have specific meanings. The prefix **re-** means again. If **re-** is added to the beginning of the root **write,** it makes the new word **rewrite** (to write again). The suffix **-er** indicates a person. Added to the end of the root **write,** it makes the new word **writer** (a person who writes).

In this workbook you will study some prefixes and some suffixes. There are many more. These prefixes and suffixes will help you recognize different words that can be made from one basic root. **Do not attempt to make new words yourself.** If you add prefixes or suffixes to word-roots, your new words may not be words people use. Do not use a word-form unless you have seen it in your reading.

Did you understand what you read about roots, prefixes, and suffixes? Fill in the blank in each sentence to find out.

1. A _____ is added to the front of the root.

2. A _____ is added to the end of a root.

3. The basic part of a word to which you add prefixes and suffixes

   is called a _____.

4. In the word **unapproachable,** "un" is probably a _____.

5. In the word **unapproachable,** "approach" is probably a

   _____.

6. In the word **unapproachable,** "able" is probably a

   _____.

Prefixes to Know	Prefixes (word-beginnings) come at the beginning of a word. They change the meaning of a word and sometimes may change a word from one part of speech to another part. Learning these word-beginnings can help you build new words and make new meanings.

In this list, prefixes will be in groups according to their meanings.

In, into	**in-, im-**	
	inhale (v)	**in** + hale means to breathe in.
	imprison (v)	**im** + prison means to put into prison.
		(*Note:* **in-** becomes **im-** before the letters **b, m,** and **p.**)
	en-, em-	
	enslave (v)	**en** + slave means to put into slavery, to make a slave of.
	embrace (v)	**em** + brace means to hug; to take into one's arms; to hold in your arms. (The root **brace** means arm.)
		(*Note:* **en-** becomes **em-** before **b, m,** and **p.**)
Out	**e-, ex-**	
	exhale (v)	**ex** + hale means to breathe out.
To, toward	**ad-**	
	advance (v)	**ad** + vance means to go forward; to go toward.

Away, from	**ab-**	
	abduct (v)	**ab** + duct means to lead away by force; kidnap.
	de-	
	defend (v)	**de** + fend means to keep the enemy away from; to protect.
Not	**un-**	
	uneducated (adj)	**un** + educated means not educated.
Take away, not, lack	**dis-**	
	disarm (v)	**dis** + arm means to take away a weapon.
With, along with, together	**con-, com-, co-**	
	conversation (n)	**con** + versation means talking with one or more people.
	cooperate (v)	**co** + operate means to work along with others.
Back, again	**re-**	
	return (v)	**re** + turn means to turn back.
	remarry (v)	**re** + marry means to marry again.

Did you understand? Fill in the blanks with the correct prefix or word.

1. The prefix in the word **rehire** is _____. It means _____.

2. The prefix in the word **absent** is _____. It means _____.

3. The prefix in the word **unloving** is _____. It means _____.

4. The prefix in the word **disagree** is _____. It means _____.

5. The prefix in the word **entrance** is _____. It means _____.

Match the prefix with its meaning.

_____ 1. ad-   a. again

_____ 2. en-   b. with, together

_____ 3. de-   c. to, toward

_____ 4. re-   d. not

_____ 5. con-   e. away, from

_____ 6. un-   f. in, into

Suffixes to Know

Suffixes (word-endings) come at the end of a word. They show whether the word is a verb, noun, adjective, or adverb. Learning these word-endings can help you recognize a verb, noun, adjective, or adverb.

Verb Endings	**-en**	at the end of a word means to make _____.
	brighten (v)	bright + **en** means to make bright.
	soften (v)	soft + **en** means to make soft.
	-ize	at the end of a word means to make _____.
	publicize (v)	public + **ize** means to make public, or to make the public aware of.
Noun Endings	**-ment**	at the end of a word means act of _____; state of _____; result of _____.
	contentment (n)	content + **ment** means the state of being satisfied (content).
	-sion, -tion	at the end of a word means act of _____; state of _____.
	celebration (n)	celebrate + **tion** means the act of celebrating.
	-ness	at the end of a word means state of _____.
	toughness (n)	tough + **ness** means the state of being tough.
	-ance, -ence	at the end of a word means act of _____; state of _____; quality of _____.
	assistance (n)	assist + **ance** means act of giving help.
	-er, -or	at the end of a word means one who _____; that which _____.
	fighter (n)	fight + **er** means one who fights.
	actor (n)	act + **or** means one who acts.
	-ist	at the end of a word also means one who _____; that which _____.
	violinist (n)	violin + **ist** means one who plays the violin.
Adjective Endings	**-en**	at the end of a word means made of _____.
	wooden (adj)	wood + **en** means made of wood. *Note:* When the word is an adjective, the **-en** means made of _____. We have seen **-en** at the end of a verb. There it means to make _____.
	-ic	at the end of a word means characteristic of _____; like _____.
	heroic (adj)	hero + **ic** means characteristic of a hero.
	poetic (adj)	poet + **ic** means characteristic of (or like) poets or poetry.

-al	sometimes makes an adjective; when it makes an adjective it means relating to _____.
financial (adj)	finance + **al** means relating to finance. (**Finance** means **money**.)
manual (adj)	manu + **al** means relating to the hand. (**Manus** means **hand** in Latin.)
-able	at the end of a word means able _____; can _____; or giving _____.
portable (adj)	port + **able** means can be carried; able to be carried.
pleasurable (adj)	pleasure + **able** means giving pleasure.
-y	at the end of a word means having _____.
hairy (adj)	hair + **y** means having hair (a lot of hair).
rainy (adj)	rain + **y** means having rain.
-ous	at the end of a word means full of _____; having _____.
mysterious (adj)	mystery + **ous** means full of mystery.
-ful	at the end of a word means full of _____; having _____.
hopeful (adj)	hope + **ful** means full of hope.
beautiful (adj)	beauty + **ful** means full of beauty. *Note:* The suffix **-ful** is always spelled with one **l**; the word **full** has two.
-less	at the end of a word means without _____.
powerless (adj)	power + **less** means without power.
homeless (adj)	home + **less** means without a home.
Adverb Endings **-ly**	at the end of a word almost always makes an adverb; occasionally it will make an adjective.
quickly (adv)	quick + **ly**.

Did you understand? Fill in each blank, and circle the correct part of speech.

1. The suffix in the word **legalize** is _____. It makes the word a (an):

    n   v   adj   adv

2. The suffix in the word **seriousness** is _____. It makes the word a (an):

    n   v   adj   adv

3. The suffix in the word **educator** is _____. It makes the word a (an):

    n   v   adj   adv

4. The suffix in the word **marginal** is _____. It makes the word a (an):

    n   v   adj   adv

5. The suffix in the word **loveable** is _____. It makes the word a (an):

    n   v   adj   adv

Underline the word which corroctly completes each sentence.

1. A _____ is a person who teaches.

    teach   teaching   teacher

2. A _____ person is one without fear.

    fearful   fearless   fearlessness   fearfulness

3. On a _____ day there is a lot of sun.

    sun   sunny   sunshine

4. A _____ story is full of humor.

    humor   humorous   humorously

5. A new driver drives very _____.

    careful   carefully   carefulness

Prefixes and Suffixes to Learn	A prefix comes at the beginning of a word, and a suffix at the end

Prefixes to Know	in-, im-	in; into
	en-, em-	in; into
	e-, ex-	out; out of
	ad-	to; toward
	ab-	away; from
	de-	away; from
	un-	not
	dis-	take away; not; lack
	con-, com-, co-	with; along with; together
	re-	back; again

Suffixes to Know

Suffixes that make verbs

-en	to make _____
-ize	to make_____

Suffixes that make nouns

-ment	act of _____; state of _____
-sion, -tion	act of _____; state of _____
-ness	state of _____
-ance, -ence	action, state, quality of _____
-er, -or	one who _____; that which _____
-ist	one who _____; that which _____

Suffixes that make adjectives

-en	made of _____
-ic	characteristic of _____; like _____
-al	relating to _____
-able	able; can; giving
-y	having _____
-ous	full of _____; having _____
-ful	full of _____; having _____
-less	without _____

Suffix that makes adverbs

-ly

PARTS OF SPEECH

To use English words correctly, you must know something about English sentences and the parts of speech. The four most important parts of speech to know in English are: verb (v), noun (n), adjective (adj), and adverb (adv). In this lesson you will learn how to know the parts of speech.

Subject and Verb

Every sentence in English must have a subject and a verb.

Verbs

Most **verbs** are action words. Some examples of verbs are: hit, run, swim, skate, jump, fly, and move. The verb tells what is happening in a sentence. To find the verb, ask the question: **Do** or **does what?**

Example: Danny swims. (Danny **does what?** Swims. **Swims** is the verb.)

Example: Jenny is studying English. (Jenny is **doing what?** Is studying. **Is studying** is the verb.)

The most common verb in English is the verb to be. It is not really an action word, but it is always a verb. The forms of this verb are: **am, is, are, was, were, be, being, been.**

Subjects

The **subject** is the person or thing doing the action. The subject is the **doer.** To find the subject, ask the question: **Who** or **what + verb?**

Example: Roberto sings. (**Who** sings? Roberto. **Roberto** is the subject.)

Example: The big bear ate the fish. (**What** ate? Bear. **Bear** is the subject.)

Example: The ball fell at his feet. (**What** fell? Ball. **Ball** is the subject.)

Roberto, bear, and **ball** are the subjects of these sentences. They are **nouns**. A noun is the name of a person, place, or thing.

We could also use **pronouns** in the sentences. The subject must be a noun or a pronoun. A pronoun takes the place of a noun.

Example: **He** sings. (**He** takes the place of **Roberto**.)

Example: **It** ate the fish. (**It** takes the place of **bear**.)

Example: **It** fell at his feet. (**It** takes the place of **ball**.)

The subjects in these sentences—he, it, it—are pronouns.

Remember: 1. The verb is the **action word**.
2. The subject is the **doer** of the action.
3. The subject must be a noun or pronoun.
4. A noun is the name of a person, place, or thing.
5. A pronoun takes the place of a noun.

Try this exercise.

Write **s** under the **subject** and **v** under the **verb** of each sentence. Some verbs can be more than one word (for example: is running, will be taking, etc.).

1. The little girl ate the awful food.

2. Did the bee sting you?

3. The young couple ran along the beach.

4. Everyone wanted an ice cream cone on that hot day.

5. Is the phone book in the car?

Objects

In English there are two kinds of objects:

> the object of a verb
> the object of a preposition.

An English sentence may have one or both of these kinds of objects. The sentence may have no object at all.

Object of a Verb

The **object of a verb** is the receiver of the action of a verb. To find the object of a verb, ask the question: (verb) + **what** or **whom?**

Example: Manuel hit the ball. (Hit **what?** Ball. **Ball** is the object.)

Example: Sue lost the keys to her car. (Lost **what?** Keys. **Keys** is the object.)

Example: Kim saw me yesterday. (Saw **whom?** Me. **Me** is the object.)

Ball and **keys** are nouns; **me** is a pronoun.
The object of a verb must be a noun or pronoun.

Object of a Preposition

There are many prepositions in English. Most prepositions show direction or position (in, on, at, by, after, below, etc.). Other prepositions show the relationship between people or things (with, of, etc.).

A preposition must go with a noun to make a phrase. The phrase contains the preposition and its object. The object completes the thought of the phrase.

To find the object of a preposition, ask the question: (preposition) **what** or **whom?**

Example: I walked to school. (To **what?** School. **School** is the object of the preposition **to**.)

Example: Fred went with me to the game. (With **whom?** Me. **Me** is the object of the preposition **with**.) (To **what?** Game. **Game** is the object of the preposition **to**.)

School and **game** are nouns; **me** is a pronoun. The object of a preposition must be a noun or pronoun.

Note: Do not confuse the preposition **to** with the infinitive marker **to**. The preposition **to** goes with a noun. The infinitive marker **to** goes with a verb.

preposition + noun

Example: He went to school to study.

infinitive marker + verb

Practice what you have learned.	Write **s** under the subject, **v** under the verb, **o** under the object of the verb, and **op** under the object of a preposition. Remember that the verb may be more than one word.

1. The quick brown fox bit the lazy dog.

2. Sara is playing the piano with her mother.

3. Did you fix the broken chair?

4. The discovery of oil in Alaska helped the United States.

5. Terry memorized the words for his Spanish lesson.

Adjectives

Adjectives give information or tell about nouns. (They describe or modify nouns.) To find an adjective, ask one of several questions: **which** (noun)**?** or **what kind of** (noun)**?** or **how many** (nouns)**?** Look at this sentence:

The little boy licked his big yellow lollipop.

(**Which** boy**?** The little boy. **The** and **little** are adjectives.)

(**Which** lollipop**?** His big yellow lollipop. **His**, **big**, and **yellow** are adjectives.)

Notice: **The** is a special kind of adjective. It is called an article. In English we have two articles, **a** (**an**) and **the**. They are always followed by a noun, but sometimes other adjectives will come between the article and the noun. You see this in our example sentence:

adjective
↓
The little boy
↗   ↖
article   noun

His is another special kind of adjective. It shows ownership or possession. Other possessive adjectives are: **my**, **your**, **her**, **his**, **our**, **its**, and **their**.

In English, adjectives usually come before the noun they tell about.

Adverbs

Adverbs give information about verbs or adjectives. To find an adverb, ask the question: **How** (adjective)**?** or (verb) **how?**

Example: The very large bird flew quickly to its nest.

(**Which** bird**?** The large bird. **Large** is an adjective.)

(**How** large**?** Very large. **Very** is an adverb.)

(Flew **how?** Flew quickly. **Quickly** is an adverb.)

A few adverbs also answer other questions. For example, **when?** (yesterday, later, now, tomorrow, etc.) or **where?** (here, there, far, etc.)

How to Know the Part of Speech of a Word

Word Forms

In English a word will often change its form when it changes its part of speech.

Example: She is a **beautiful** girl. She sings **beautifully**.
  (adj)   (adv)

Example: Few people **live** 100 years. **Life** is too short.
  (verb)   (noun)

In *Working on Words* you will study many suffixes. They will give you a clue about the part of speech of a word. Learn each word with its part of speech, which is given in parentheses.

Word Use

Remember, the only way to be *sure* of the part of speech of a word is to know how it is used in a sentence. See how the word **jogging** can be used in different ways.

Example: Jogging is good for your health. (**Jogging** is a noun, subject of the sentence.)

Example: Alicia is jogging around the block. (**Jogging** is a verb.)

Example: The jogging man was hit by a car. (**Jogging** is an adjective.)

In English, sentences are usually written in this order:

(adjective) subject (adverb) verb (adjective) object (adverb)

(adj) + s + (adv) + v + (adj) + o + (adv)

Every sentence *must* have a subject and verb. A sentence may or may not have the other parts. Adjectives *usually* come before nouns. Adverbs are *usually* near the verb.

In Summary, Remember:

In English, the part of speech of a word depends on its use in a sentence.

If a word is the subject, it is a noun or pronoun.

If a word is an object, it is a noun or pronoun.

If a word tells about a noun, it is an adjective.

If a word tells about a verb or an adjective, it is an adverb.

Try this exercise.   Decide what part of speech each word in the sentence is. Write the
abbreviation under each word: **n** (noun), **v** (verb), **adj** (adjective),
adv (adverb), **pro** (pronoun), **prep** (preposition), or **art** (article).

Example: The little boy ate his lunch.

You answer: art adj   n   v adj   n

1. The   big   brown   dog   had   seven   puppies
    _____   _____   _____   _____   _____   _____   _____

    yesterday.

    _____

2. The   restless child   damaged   the   beautiful garden.
    _____   _____   _____   _____   _____   _____   _____

3. The   very   intelligent   girl   easily   passed   the
    _____   _____   _____   _____   _____   _____   _____

    test.

    _____

4. We   moved   slowly   to   the   beginning of
    _____   _____   _____   _____   _____   _____   _____

    the   long   line.
    _____   _____   _____

5. In   the   corner   of   the   room   was
    _____   _____   _____   _____   _____   _____   _____

    an   old   shoe.
    _____   _____   _____

(continued)

6. The soldier left the field after the

_____ _____ _____ _____ _____ _____ _____

battle.

_____

7. A lazy dog slept on the sidewalk.

_____ _____ _____ _____ _____ _____ _____

8. Did the old car travel to California?

_____ _____ _____ _____ _____ _____ _____

9. He fixed the broken bicycle quickly.

_____ _____ _____ _____ _____ _____

10. Are the students planning a trip to

_____ _____ _____ _____ _____ _____ _____

the mountains?

_____ _____

words to learn

unit 1

enjoy	enjoyable
enjoyment	pleasure
pleasant	delight
delightful	eager
enthusiastic	enthusiasm

unit 2

fault	shame
at fault	ashamed
blame	shameful
accuse	guilt
accusation	guilty

unit 3

brave	coward
bravery	cowardly
courage	cowardice
courageous	fearless
bold	boldness

unit 4

flame	inflame
blaze	flammable
flare	ignite
scorch	arson
glow	arsonist

unit 5

regard	disregard
respect	disrespect
honor	resent
admire	jealous
worship	jealousy

units 1-5 pretest

Matching

Match each word with a word that means the same or almost the same. Make sure that the words are the same part of speech (noun, verb, adjective, adverb).

Unit
Key

(1) _____	1. enthusiastic	a. courage
(2) _____	2. guilty	b. at fault
(4) _____	3. blaze	c. enjoyable
(3) _____	4. bold	d. ignore
(5) _____	5. respect	e. fearless
(5) _____	6. disregard	f. pleasure
(3) _____	7. bravery	g. fire
(1) _____	0. pleasant	h. accuse
(2) _____	9. blame	i. honor
(1) _____	10. delight	j. scorch
		k. eager

Sentences

Write one sentence of your own for each word here.

Unit
Key

(1) 1. enthusiasm _____

_____

(2) 2. blame _____

_____

(4) 3. ignite _____

_____

(1) 4. eager _____

_____

(3) 5. cowardly _____

_____

(2) 6. accuse _____

_____

(5) 7. admire _____

_____

(4) 8. arson _____

_____

(5) 9. resent _____

_____

(2) 10. ashamed _____

_____

Teacher's Comments:

Units to be Done: 1   2   3   4   5

unit 1

words to learn

enjoy
enjoyment
pleasant
delightful
enthusiastic

enjoyable
pleasure
delight
eager
enthusiasm

Definitions and Examples

Joy means *happiness.*

enjoy*
(v)

To **enjoy** means to feel happy when you do something.

Example: Maria and Jose **enjoy** playing tennis.

enjoyable
(adj)

Something you enjoy is **enjoyable.**

Example: Maria and Jose think that tennis is **enjoyable.**

enjoyment
(n)

Enjoyment is the happiness you feel when you do something. Something you enjoy gives you **enjoyment.**

Example: Maria and Jose play tennis for **enjoyment.**

pleasure
(n)

Pleasure means enjoyment.

Example: Maria and Jose play tennis for **pleasure.**

pleasant
(adj)

Pleasant means enjoyable.

Example: Maria and Jose think that playing tennis is **pleasant**.

delight
(v, n)

To **delight** (v) means to make someone happy.

Example: Tennis **delights** Maria and Jose.

Delight (n) means joy, happiness, enjoyment, pleasure.

Example: Maria and Jose think that playing tennis is a **delight**.

delightful (adj)	**Delightful** means enjoyable, pleasant. *Example:* Maria and Jose think that playing tennis is a **delightful** activity.
eager* (adj)	**Eager** means you really want to do something very much. *Example:* Maria and Jose are **eager** to play tennis today.
enthusiastic* (adj)	**Enthusiastic** means eager. *Example:* Maria and Jose are **enthusiastic** about tennis. *Example:* Maria and Jose are **enthusiastic** about playing tennis.
enthusiasm* (n)	**Enthusiasm** is an eager feeling, a feeling that you really want to do something very much. *Example:* Maria and Jose have a lot of **enthusiasm** for tennis. *Example:* Maria and Jose have a lot of **enthusiasm** for playing tennis.

*To use these words correctly, you need to know these patterns.

1. The words **enthusiastic** and **enthusiasm** follow these patterns:

> enthusiastic + about + noun
>
> enthusiastic + about + verb + -ing
>
> enthusiasm + for + noun
>
> enthusiasm + for + verb + -ing

Examples: We are not enthusiastic **about baseball**.
We are not enthusiastic **about playing** baseball.
We have no enthusiasm **for baseball**.
We have no enthusiasm **for playing** baseball.

We do not usually say "have enthusiasm." We need something between these two words.

Examples: We have **great** enthusiasm for baseball.
We have **little** enthusiasm for baseball.

2. The verb **enjoy** must follow this pattern:

> enjoy + noun
>
> enjoy + verb + -ing

Examples: John enjoys **movies**.
John enjoys **going** to the movies.

3. The word **eager** must follow this pattern:

> eager + to + verb

Example: Curtis is eager **to pass** this course.

Fill in each blank with one of these words.

enjoy   pleasant   eager
enjoyable   delight   enthusiastic
enjoyment   delightful   enthusiasm
pleasure

1. I _____ going to the movies.

2. *The Wizard of Oz* is a (an) _____ children's movie.

3. Children's movies sometimes _____ adults, too.

4. Even today young children are _____ to see it.

5. Their greatest _____ is when the wicked witch is killed.

6. Many parents are _____ about seeing the movie again.

7. All in all it is a (an) _____ experience.

Word-Roots, Word-Beginnings (Prefixes), and Word-Endings (Suffixes)

Look at these words. See how the word-endings make new words.

delightful   delight + **ful** means **full of delight.** (**-ful** makes an adjective.)

enjoyable   enjoy + **able** means **giving joy.** (**-able** makes an adjective.)

enjoyment   enjoy + **ment** means **action of enjoying.** (**-ment** makes a noun.)

enthusiastic   enthusiasm + **tic** means **full of enthusiasm.** (**-ic** makes an adjective. We drop the **m** and add **t**.)

Related Words	enjoy (v)	delight (v)	please (v)
	enjoyment (n)	delight (n)	pleasure (n)
	enjoyable (adj)	delightful (adj)	pleasurable (adj)
			pleasant (adj)
		delightfully (adv)	pleasantly (adv)

	eagerness (n)	enthusiasm (n)
	eager (adj)	enthusiastic (adj)
	eagerly (adv)	enthusiastically (adv)

Note: the prefix **un-** means **not**.

unenjoyable (adj)	unpleasant (adj)	unenthusiastic (adj)
	unpleasantly (adv)	unenthusiastically (adv)

Using These Words

Circle the correct word in each pair.

enjoy (v)

pleasure (n)

delightful (adj)

enjoyable (adj)

pleasant (adj)

eager (adj)

enthusiasm (n)

enjoyment (n)

delight (v, n)

enthusiastic (adj)

Margo (enjoys/is eager) learning languages. She is now studying

French with great (enthusiasm/enthusiastic). Margo thinks that studying

languages is a very (pleasure/enjoyable) activity, and she always does it

with a lot of (enthusiasm/enthusiastic). Margo's friends do not understand

why French gives her so much (pleasant/pleasure), but Margo is very

(eager/enthusiastic) about studying it. She is very (eager/enthusiasm)

to learn French well.

Read this story.

John loves baseball. He is a very good baseball player. He plays baseball almost every day. He thinks baseball is a lot of fun and very good exercise.

We can write the following sentences about this story:

John **enjoys** playing baseball.

John thinks that baseball is very **enjoyable**.

Baseball gives John a lot of **enjoyment**.

Baseball gives John a lot of **delight**.

Baseball gives John a lot of **pleasure**.

John thinks that baseball is **delightful**.

John thinks that baseball is very **pleasant**.

John is **enthusiastic** about baseball.

John is **eager** to play baseball.

John plays baseball with a lot of **enthusiasm**.

Write three sentences about each of the following stories. Use some of the new words from this unit.

enjoy (v)

pleasure (n)

delightful (adj)

enjoyable (adj)

pleasant (adj)

eager (adj)

enthusiasm (n)

enjoyment (n)

delight (v, n)

enthusiastic (adj)

a. Mark loves football. He loves to play it, and he loves to watch it, too. During the football season, he goes to see a game every weekend.

1. _____

_____

2. _____

_____

3. _____

_____

b. Mr. Chan loves to play cards. He spends all of his free time playing cards with his friends.

1. _____

_____

2. _____

_____

3. _____

_____

enjoy (v)

pleasure (n)

delightful (adj)

enjoyable (adj)

pleasant (adj)

eager (adj)

enthusiasm (n)

enjoyment (n)

delight (v, n)

enthusiastic (adj)

c. Reading mystery stories is Darryl's favorite activity. Every time he feels bored, he reads a mystery story. He always feels very happy when he reads a mystery story.

1. _____

_____

_____

2. _____

_____

_____

3. _____

_____

d. Mel's grandmother loves to bake. She bakes a cake or some cookies every day. Baking is her hobby. She always feels good when she is baking. Baking is her favorite activity.

1. _____

_____

_____

2. _____

_____

3. _____

_____

_____

enjoy (v)

pleasure (n)

delightful (adj)

enjoyable (adj)

pleasant (adj)

eager (adj)

enthusiasm (n)

enjoyment (n)

delight (v, n)

enthusiastic (adj)

e. Raquel hates to sew. She is terrible at sewing. Every time she must sew something, she feels very unhappy.

1. _____

_____

_____

2. _____

_____

_____

3. _____

_____

_____

Write one story (five to seven sentences) using **five** or more of the new words you have learned. Use any of the stories in this unit as an example.

_____

_____

_____

_____

_____

_____

_____

_____

_____

_____

unit 2

words to learn

fault	shame
at fault	ashamed
blame	shameful
accuse	guilt
accusation	guilty

Definitions and Examples

fault
(n)

If you do a bad thing, that bad thing is your **fault.**

Example: Gary got angry and hit his little sister in the eye. Her injured eye was Gary's **fault.**

at fault
(adj)

When you do a bad thing, you are **at fault.** It is your **fault.**

Example: His little sister's eye was injured, and Gary was **at fault.**

blame*
(v)

To **blame** means to say that someone did a bad thing or to say that someone is at fault.

Example: Gary's mother **blamed** him for hurting his little sister's eye.

accuse*
(v)

To **accuse** means to blame.

Example: Gary's mother **accused** him of hurting his little sister's eye.

accusation
(n)

Accusation means saying someone is at fault.

Example: Gary started to cry when he heard his mother's **accusation.**

Fill in each blank with one of these words.

fault   accuse   blame
at fault   accusation

1. They always _____ Joe of stealing apples.

2. Raul did not study. It was his own _____ that he failed.

3. Naomi's mother thought that Naomi had eaten the cake she had made for dinner. She said, "Naomi, you ate my cake." She made

   that _____ because Naomi's face was covered with frosting.

4. Naomi's mother did _____ her for eating the cake.

5. Naomi did eat the cake. She was _____.

shame (n)	A person who feels very bad for doing a bad thing feels **shame.** *Example:* The **shame** of flunking out of school made Fred afraid to call his old school friends.
ashamed (adj)	A person who feels very bad for doing a bad thing is **ashamed.** *Example:* The small boy was **ashamed** of hurting his sister. A person can be **ashamed** of himself, his actions, or of someone close to him. *Example:* The coach was **ashamed** of his team's performance.
guilt* (n)	A person who feels very bad for doing a bad thing feels **guilt. Guilt** is also the legal responsibility for breaking the law. *Example:* After the accident, the driver's **guilt** kept her awake nights. *Example:* They accused Joe of stealing apples, and the evidence proved his **guilt.**
guilty* (adj)	A person is **guilty** when he makes something bad happen, or does something bad. *Example:* Samuel was found **guilty** of murder.
shameful (adj)	The bad thing you do is **shameful.** *Example:* Stealing is a **shameful** thing to do.

✱To use these words correctly, you need to know these things.

guilty   When a person does something bad or makes something bad happen, we say that person is **guilty.** People can **feel guilty** when they have not actually done anything bad.

Example: Karen and Bill went to a store. Karen saw Bill steal a pencil. Bill is **guilty** of stealing the pencil. Karen **feels guilty** because she did not stop Bill.

guilt   Guilt is also used in these two ways. A person can **feel** a lot of **guilt** for something he did not do. Also, we may say, "I feel **no** guilt," or "I feel **a lot of** guilt." We do *not* say,

~~"I feel guilt."~~ We say, "I feel guilty."

Fill in each blank with one of these words.

shame   guilty   guilt
ashamed   shameful

1. Eric should be _____ of himself.

2. Eric is _____ of sleeping until noon every day.

3. Eric missed his class, but he feels no _____.

4. Some people think that sleeping until noon is _____.

5. Eric missed a test. He feels a lot of _____ about that now.

Word-Roots
Word-Beginnings
(Prefixes),
and Word-Endings
(Suffixes)

Look at these words. See how the word-endings make new words.

shameful   shame + **ful** means **full of shame.** (**-ful** makes an adjective.)

accusation   accuse + **tion** means **action of accusing.** (**-tion** makes a noun.)

guilty   guilt + **y** means **having guilt.** (**-y** makes an adjective.)

Related Words

shame (v)		accuse (v)
shame (n)	guilt (n)	accusation (n)
		accuser (n)
shameful (adj)	guilty (adj)	
ashamed (adj)		
shamefully (adv)		
fault (n)		
at fault (adj)		

Using These Words
Circle the correct word in each pair.

fault (n)
accuse (v)
ashamed (adj)
at fault (adj)
accusation (n)
guilt (n)
guilty (adj)
blame (v)
shame (n)
shameful (adj)

Mr. Smith took his car to a mechanic last week for some repairs. The mechanic did very bad work on the car. This week Mr. Smith's car broke down on his way to New York for a very important business meeting. Mr. Smith (accused/blamed) the mechanic of doing bad work. He said that the mechanic was (accusation/at fault). The mechanic, however, did not feel (guilty/fault) about it. He said that it was not his (fault/at fault). But Mr. Smith said that the mechanic's poor work was (ashamed/shameful) and that the mechanic should be (ashamed/shameful) of himself. The mechanic said that he felt no (guilt/guilty) and that Mr. Smith's (accuse/accusation) was not true.

Read this story.

Tony was driving his car. He was not watching the road. He was looking at the people on the sidewalk. He hit a parked car.

We can write the following sentences about this story:

The police said that this accident was Tony's **fault.**

The police **accused** Tony of causing this accident.

Their **accusation** was that Tony caused the accident.

The police **blamed** Tony for this accident.

The police said that Tony was **guilty.**

The police said that Tony was **at fault** in this accident.

We can also write the following sentences about this story:

Tony was **ashamed** of driving so carelessly.

Tony felt great **shame** for driving so carelessly.

Tony's careless driving was **shameful.**

Tony felt **guilty** about driving so carelessly.

Tony had a feeling of **guilt** about driving so carelessly.

Write three sentences about each of the following stories. Use some of the new words from this unit. You may also use words from the first unit.

a. Mrs. Jones was smoking in bed. She fell asleep. A fire started. Nobody was hurt, but the house was badly burned.

1. _____

_____

2. _____

_____

3. _____

_____

fault (n)

accuse (v)

ashamed (adj)

at fault (adj)

accusation (n)

guilt (n)

guilty (adj)

blame (v)

shame (n)

shameful (adj)

b. Carlos has class at 8:00 a.m. Roger wakes him up every day at 7:30 a.m. This morning Roger forgot to wake Carlos up, and Carlos missed his class.

1. _____

_____

2. _____

_____

3. _____

_____

fault (n)
accuse (v)
ashamed (adj)
at fault (adj)
accusation (n)
guilt (n)
guilty (adj)
blame (v)
shame (n)
shameful (adj)

c. Andy plays football at college. During the game last Saturday, Andy was very careless and fumbled the ball three times. His team lost the game because of Andy's carelessness.

1. _____

_____

_____

2. _____

_____

_____

3. _____

_____

_____

d. Gloria did not lock her car last night. She had a very expensive coat in the car. A thief stole the coat.

1. _____

_____

_____

2. _____

_____

_____

3. _____

_____

_____

| fault (n) |
| accuse (v) |
| ashamed (adj) |
| at fault (adj) |
| accusation (n) |
| guilt (n) |
| guilty (adj) |
| blame (v) |
| shame (n) |
| shameful (adj) |

e. Mr. Vincento was cooking a delicious dinner. His roast was in the oven. He began to read a book. He completely forgot about his roast until he smelled something burning. His delicious dinner was ruined.

1. _____

_____

_____

2. _____

_____

_____

3. _____

_____

_____

Write your own story (five to seven sentences). Use **five** or more of the new words or related words you have learned.

_____

_____

_____

_____

_____

_____

_____

_____

_____

unit 3

brave	coward
bravery	cowardly
courage	cowardice
courageous	fearless
bold	boldness

Definitions and Examples

brave
(adj)

Brave means you know something may hurt you, but you go ahead and face it.

Example: Alex is a **brave** man. He's not afraid of danger.

bravery
(n)

When you show that you have no worry about being hurt, you show your **bravery**.

Example: All Alex's friends talk about his **bravery**.

courage
(n)

Courage means bravery.

Example: All Alex's friends talk about Alex's **courage**.

courageous
(adj)

Courageous means brave.

Example: Alex is a **courageous** person.

boldness
(n)

Boldness means courage, bravery.

Example: All Alex's friends talk about his **boldness**.

bold
(adj)

Bold means courageous, brave.

Example: Alex is a **bold** person.

fearless
(adj)

Fearless means bold, courageous, brave, or without fear.

Example: Alex is a **fearless** person.

Fill in each blank with one of these words.

brave	courageous	bold
bravery	boldness	fearless
courage		

1. A mother took her daughter to the dentist. She said, "Be

   _____. He won't hurt you."

2. A person who is not afraid of anything is _____.

3. The child's _____ saved her pet's life.

4. The Pilgrims had the _____ to travel across the ocean.

---

coward (n)	A **coward** is a person who is always worried that something will hurt him.
cowardly (adj)	A person who is always worried about being hurt is a **cowardly** person.
cowardice (n)	When a person shows a feeling that he is always worried about being hurt, he shows his **cowardice**.

Fill in each blank with one of these words.

coward	cowardly	cowardice

1. The _____ was afraid to defend himself.

2. I could have become a police officer, but my

   _____ prevented me. I was afraid of getting killed!

3. The _____ dog ran away from the kitten.

**Word-Roots,
Word-Beginnings
(Prefixes),
and Word-Endings
(Suffixes)**

Look at these words. See how the word-endings make new words.

cowardly   coward + **ly** means **like a coward.** (**-ly** makes an adjective here. Usually it makes an adverb.)

fearless   fear + **less** means **without fear.** (**-less** makes an adjective.)

boldness   bold + **ness** means **state of being bold.** (**-ness** makes a noun.)

courageous   courage + **ous** means **full of courage.** (**-ous** makes an adjective.)

The root **-cour-** is interesting to know about. It means heart. A person with courage has heart. A **courageous** person is a person full of heart. This root gives us the verbs to **encourage**, meaning to **put heart into** and to **discourage**, meaning to **take heart away from.**

Related Words

brave (v)		
bravery (n)	courage (n)	boldness (n)
brave (adj)	courageous (adj)	bold (adj)
	courageously (adv)	boldly (adv)
		discourage (v)
fearlessness (n)	coward (n)	discouragement (n)
	cowardice (n)	
fearless (adj)	cowardly (adj)	discouraging (adj)
fearlessly (adv)		

Using These Words
Circle the correct word from each pair.

brave (adj)

bravery (n)

fearless (adj)

courage (n)

courageous (adj)

bold (adj)

boldness (n)

coward (n)

cowardice (n)

cowardly (adj)

Police officers have a very dangerous job. A (brave/cowardly) person could not be one. A police officer must have a lot of (courage/courageous) on the job. My friend Juan is a police officer. He is very (bravery/courageous). Last week he was chasing a criminal. The criminal pulled out a gun and shot at Juan. Juan did not stop. He continued to follow the criminal. Finally Juan caught him. Juan was not afraid. All of Juan's friends were proud of his (boldness/fearless), and Juan got a medal for his (bravery/bold). A (cowardice/coward) would not be a good police officer. Police officers must face danger with (brave/courage) every day.

Read this story.

Sergeant Murphy was a hero in World War II. During an attack, the enemy soldiers surrounded him. He grabbed a machine gun and stood there firing all around him. Alone, without any help, he killed many enemy soldiers.

We can say that:

Sergeant Murphy was very **brave**.

Sergeant Murphy was very **courageous**.

Sergeant Murphy was very **fearless**.

Sergeant Murphy was very **bold**.

or

Sergeant Murphy showed great **courage**.

Sergeant Murphy showed great **boldness**.

Sergeant Murphy showed great **bravery**.

Read this story.

The young soldier was always worried about going into battle. He was worried that an enemy soldier would kill him. When his group went into battle, he ran away. The Military Police found him and executed (killed) him for not doing his duty.

We can say that:

Some people think that the young soldier was a **coward**.

Some people think that the young soldier's actions were **cowardly**.

Some people think that the young soldier showed **cowardice** when he ran away.

brave (adj)

bravery (n)

fearless (adj)

courage (n)

courageous (adj)

bold (adj)

boldness (n)

coward (n)

cowardice (n)

cowardly (adj)

Write three sentences about each of the following stories. Use some of the new words from this unit. You may also use words from past units.

a. Ed Johnson is a fire fighter. Last week he saved a little girl from a fire in her home. He rushed into the burning house and stayed there until he found her.

1. _____

_____

_____

2. _____

_____

_____

3. _____

_____

_____

brave (adj)

bravery (n)

fearless (adj)

courage (n)

courageous (adj)

bold (adj)

boldness (n)

coward (n)

cowardice (n)

cowardly (adj)

b. Reuben joined the army last month. He wants to become a parachute jumper. He knows that this is very dangerous. He knows he could get hurt, but he is not afraid.

1. _____

_____

_____

2. _____

_____

_____

3. _____

_____

c. Texas Tillie is a famous rodeo star. She rides wild horses in the rodeo. She has fallen from the horses many times and has broken many bones in her body. But she still loves the rodeo and is not afraid of her dangerous job.

1. _____

_____

_____

2. _____

_____

_____

3. _____

_____

_____

brave (adj)

bravery (n)

fearless (adj)

courage (n)

courageous (adj)

bold (adj)

boldness (n)

coward (n)

cowardice (n)

cowardly (adj)

d. The pioneers who settled in the western United States in the nineteenth century had to face many dangers. They fought and killed Indians and wild animals. They lived in poor houses and did very hard work. They had a hard and dangerous life, but they were not afraid.

1. _____

_____

_____

2. _____

_____

_____

3. _____

_____

_____

e. Fred was a soldier in Viet Nam during the war. In 1967, the North Vietnamese captured him. They tried to make Fred tell them military secrets. They beat Fred often. They said that they would kill him if he did not talk, but Fred never told them anything.

1. _____

_____

_____

2. _____

_____

_____

3. _____

_____

_____

Write your own story (five to seven sentences). Use **five** or more new words you have learned in this unit.

brave (adj)

bravery (n)

fearless (adj)

courage (n)

courageous (adj)

bold (adj)

boldness (n)

coward (n)

cowardice (n)

cowardly (adj)

_____

_____

_____

_____

_____

_____

_____

_____

_____

_____

unit 4

words to learn

flame	inflame
blaze	flammable
flare	ignite
scorch	arson
glow	arsonist

Definitions and Examples

flame
(n)

A **flame** is the tip (or tongue) of red or yellow light that rises above a fire.

Example: **Flames** from the fireplace warmed his cold hands.

Example: When he dropped the match, the pile of old newspapers burst into **flames**.

blaze
(v, n)

To **blaze** (v) means to burn brightly, strongly, quickly.

Example: The fire in the paint factory **blazed** for three days.

A **blaze** (n) is a strongly burning fire.

Example: Fire fighters could not put out the **blaze**.

flare
(v, n)

To **flare** (v) is to blaze with a sudden, bright light; **flare** also means to burst out suddenly in anger (often used with **up**—to **flare up**).

Example: First one fire then another **flared** in the night.

Example: Don't **flare up** at me just because you lost your job!

A **flare** (n) is a bright burst of light lasting only a short time. **Flare** also is the name for the torch-like bright light you set out by your car in emergency situations.

Example: Police suggest that you always have a **flare** in your trunk in case of an emergency on the highway.

scorch (v)	To **scorch** is to burn something a little and make it black or brown on the outside. *Example:* The strong July sun **scorched** all the lawns in my hometown.
glow (v)	To **glow** is to burn low, steady, and warm, but without flames; to give off light. *Example:* Even at 2:00 in the morning the log still **glowed** in the fireplace. *Example:* Fireflies **glow** in the night.
inflame (v)	To **inflame** means to make swollen, red, sore (as if filled with fire). *Example:* The doctor told her patient that he had **inflamed** the insect bites by scratching them.
flammable (adj)	**Flammable** means capable of catching on fire (able to flame), easy to set on fire; will burn quickly (but not burning yet). *Example:* Mark read the instructions at the bottom, "Keep away from flames or heat. Highly **flammable**."
ignite* (v)	To **ignite** is to set fire to something. (It always means to begin or start or set a fire.) *Example:* Police believe that sparks from the muffler of an old truck **ignited** the forest fire that destroyed two thousand acres of Big Sur State Park.
arson (n)	**Arson** is the crime of setting fire to a building or other property. Arson is not an accident. It is always done on purpose. *Example:* A person can be sent to prison if he is found guilty of the crime of **arson**.
arsonist (n)	An **arsonist** is the person who sets fire to a building; the person who is guilty of the crime of arson. *Example:* Police accused him of being the **arsonist** who had burned two high school gyms.

*To use this word correctly, you need to know this pattern.

ignite + noun (object)

The noun (object) must be the word **fire**, **blaze**, or **flame**, or anything that can make a fire.

Examples: Joan ignited the **fire** with a match.
Blake ignited the **gasoline** by accident.

Fill in each blank with one of these words.

flame	glow	ignite
blaze	inflame	arson
flare	flammable	arsonist
scorch		

1. Gasoline is very _____.

2. A person who starts a fire in a building is a (an) _____.

3. A cigarette can _____ a fire in a trash can.

4. The candles _____ softly in the front of the church.

5. If you leave a pan on the stove too long, the heat may

   _____ it.

6. You can _____ a mosquito bite by scratching it.

7. Dry leaves _____ up as soon as a match touches them.

8. The small _____ on the candle was very hot.

9. The burning forest will _____ for a week.

10. A man was found running away from a burning store. He was

    accused of _____.

**Word-Roots,
Word-Beginnings
(Prefixes),
and Word-Endings
(Suffixes)**

You can see two suffixes in this unit: **-able** and **-ist**.

flammable   flame + **able** means **able to catch on fire** or **to burst into flames.**

arsonist   arson + **ist** means **one who sets fire; one who does arson.**

You can also see one prefix in this unit: **in-**.

inflame   **in** + flame means **fill as if with fire** or **put fire into.**

                       Example: My big toe was **in**flamed. (red and swollen)

Using These Words
Circle the correct word in each pair.

---

flame (n)

scorch (v)

flammable (adj)

blaze (v, n)

glow (v)

ignite (v)

arsonist (n)

flare (v, n)

inflame (v)

arson (v)

---

1. There was a fire in my college dorm. Police reported that the fire was not the work of an (arson/arsonist). The (blaze/scorch) was (ignited/inflamed) by a cigarette that someone had dropped near a pile of highly (flammable/flare) tissue paper. The small fire soon turned into a (flame/blaze). (Flames/Flares) spread through the fourth floor.

2. (Arson/Blaze) is the legal term (word) for the crime of burning a building or property. Punishment for the crime of (arson/blaze) varies from state to state. But the (blaze/arsonist) can be charged with murder if anyone is killed in the fire.

Read this story to see how these words can be used.

A small boy was playing with a box of matches near a pile of dry hay. The first match he struck burned his finger, and he dropped it in the hay.

We can write the following sentences to continue this story:

The match **ignited** the hay.

Flames began to rise from the hay.

Soon the whole pile was in **flames.**

The boy ran to the top of the hill and stood there watching. The fire **glowed** in his eyes.

A neighbor called the fire department to come and put out the **blaze.**

When the fire fighters arrived, the hay was completely burned, and the ground around it was **scorched.**

It was an accident. The boy was not accused of being an **arsonist.**

He was not accused of **arson.**

Write three sentences about each of the following situations. Use some of the words from this unit. You may also use words from past units.

flame (n)

scorch (v)

flammable (adj)

blaze (v, n)

glow (v)

ignite (v)

arsonist (n)

flare (v, n)

inflame (v)

arson (v)

a. The young man started a fire by deliberately dropping a burning match into the wastepaper basket. At first it was a small fire. Then the fire caught onto the drapes. Soon the entire room was on fire. He ran from the building and stood across the street. He watched the fire burning brightly.

1. _____

_____

_____

2. _____

_____

_____

3. _____

_____

_____

b. Because gasoline can easily catch on fire, you are not allowed to smoke near trucks that carry gasoline or near gasoline pumps. One careless match can start a fire that could destroy property or even hurt people.

1. _____

_____

_____

2. _____

_____

_____

3. _____

_____

_____

flame (n)

scorch (v)

flammable (adj)

blaze (v, n)

glow (v)

ignite (v)

arsonist (n)

flare (v, n)

inflame (v)

arson (v)

c. I like to start a fire in the fireplace on a cold winter night.

1. _____

_____

_____

2. _____

_____

_____

3. _____

_____

Write your own paragraph or story (five to seven sentences) using **five** or more of the new words you have learned. Use any of the paragraphs in this unit as an example.

_____

_____

_____

_____

_____

_____

_____

_____

_____

_____

_____

unit 5

words to learn	regard	disregard
	respect	disrespect
	honor	resent
	admire	jealous
	worship	jealousy

Definitions and Examples

regard
(n)

Regard is attention, concern, consideration; in the plural (**regards**) it means good wishes.

Example: You must have **regard** for your own safety.

Example: Give my **regards** to your parents when you get home.

respect
(v, n)

To **respect** (v) is to look at someone with regard or consideration; to hold in **high regard.**

Example: Children should **respect** their parents.

Respect (n) is high regard, consideration.

Example: You can show your **respect** for her by following her advice.

honor
(v, n)

To **honor** (v) is to show great respect for.

Example: The college **honored** her with an award for excellent teaching.

Honor (n) is great respect; fame, glory.

Example: It is an **honor** for a college football player to receive the Heisman Trophy.

admire
(v)

To **admire** is to look up to a person or to look at a thing with feelings of delight, pleasure, wonder; to have high regard for.

Example: I **admire** your ability to work with people of different ages.

Example: Everyone **admired** my new Mercedes.

worship
(v)

To **worship** is to take part in a religious service; to regard or honor something or someone as a deity (a god); to **worship** also means to feel strong love or admiration for.

Example: In ancient times the Romans **worshipped** Jupiter.

Example: Those students **worship** their teacher. In their eyes, she is perfect.

Fill in each blank with one of these words.

regard	admire	honor
respect	worship	

1. Winning an Oscar is a great _____ for an actor.

2. People of different religions _____ God in different ways.

3. When you go back to our old high school, give my

   _____ to Ms. Sasser.

4. I _____ anyone who can run a marathon. .

5. It is hard to work for a person you don't _____.

---

disregard
(v, n)

To **disregard** (v) is to give little or no attention to; to show little value for or regard for.

Example: Why did you **disregard** everything I advised you to do?

Example: He **disregarded** his own safety and rushed into the burning building.

Disregard (n) is lack of regard for; lack of attention to; lack of concern for.

Example: I told him to wear a tie. But he didn't. That proves his **disregard** for everything I say.

disrespect
(n)

Disrespect is lack of respect; lack of courtesy.

Example: The lawyer showed his **disrespect** for the judge by not shaking hands with her when they met later at a party.

| resent (v) | To **resent** is to feel or show bitterness toward some act or person who you feel has injured you.

Example: The child **resented** the baby-sitter for taking the toys away. |
|---|---|
| jealous (adj) | **Jealous** is to be unhappy at another person's success; to want all of another person's love or attention; to be afraid that someone you love might love someone else.

Example: I am still **jealous** of my older brother's good looks.

Example: There is nothing worse than a **jealous** husband. |
| jealousy (n) | **Jealousy** is the feeling of being jealous.

Example: I can't live with his **jealousy** any longer. |

Fill in each blank with one of these words.	disregard disrespect	jealous jealousy	resent

1. Children often _____ their brothers and sisters.

2. The old dog was _____ of the family's new pet.

3. Many people _____ the 55 m.p.h. speed limit and drive faster than that.

4. The children showed their _____ of the baby by refusing to share their toys.

5. Wearing sloppy clothes in class can be a sign of

_____ .

Word-Roots, Word-Beginnings (Prefixes), and Word-Endings (Suffixes)

You can see three prefixes in this unit: **ad-, re-,** and **dis-.** You also have two interesting roots: **-mir-** and **-spect-.**

1. The prefix **ad-** means **to.** The root **-mir-** means to **look** or to **wonder.** So the word **admire** means to **look to,** or, as people often say, to **look up to.**

We get the words **mirror** and **miracle** from this root **-mir-.**

2. You can see the prefix **re-** in the word **respect**. **Re-** means **again;** the root **-spect-** means to **look at.** So the word **respect,** which means to honor or to hold in high regard, has the idea of looking again at someone or something. In other words, when I say, "I respect your ideas," I mean that your ideas are worth a "second look."

We get the words **spectator** and **spectacular** from the root **-spect-**.

3. The third prefix in this unit is **dis-** which means **not, take away, lack.** It is a very strong *not.* With the words in this unit it means **lack of.**

Example: That shows your **disregard** for your parents (your lack of regard).

Example: That shows your **disrespect** for your parents (your lack of respect).

You can add the prefix **dis-** to one other word in this unit and make a new word. That word is **honor.** With the prefix **dis-** it becomes **dishonor.** If I **dishonor** my parents, it means that I show lack of respect for my parents or that I have taken honor away from my parents.

Related Words			
	respect (v)	admire (v)	honor (v)
	respect (n)	admiration (n)	honor (n)
		admirer (n)	
	respectable* (adj)	admirable (adj)	honorable (adj)
	respectful* (adj)		
	respectfully (adv)	admirably (adv)	honorably (adv)
	regard (v)	resent (v)	
	regard (n)	resentment (n)	jealousy (n)
		resentful (adj)	jealous (adj)
			jealously (adv)
	dishonor (v)		
	dishonor (n)		
	dishonorable (adj)	disrespectful (adj)	
	dishonorably (adv)	disrespectfully (adv)	

*A respectable person gets respect; a respectful person gives respect.

Using These Words
Circle the correct word in each pair.

regard (n)

admire (v)

disrespect (n)

respect (v, n)

worship (v)

resent (v)

jealousy (n)

honor (v, n)

disregard (v, n)

jealous (adj)

1. You (regarded/disregarded) everything I told you about him. I advised you not to date him. Remember? I said he was a very (jealous/jealousy) person. He has no (respect/resent) for you. His (jealousy/jealous) will destroy your relationship.

2. Memorial Day is a day to (honor/regard) Americans who died in wars. People show their (regard/worship) for these Americans by placing flowers or flags on their graves.

3. Long ago, the Romans used to (regard/worship) a goddess of spring and growing things. Her name was Maia. To (honor/disrespect) her and show their (admire/respect) for her, the Romans named a month of spring after Maia. They called this month *Maius.* In English it became *May.*

Read this paragraph. Notice the meaning of each new word.

A man who is **jealous** of his wife never has a moment of peace. He **resents** any talk about old boyfriends. At a party he may try to **disregard** what his wife is doing. But the minute he sees her talking to another man, he begins to wonder if she prefers that other man to him. A long time ago, people called **jealousy** the green-eyed monster, and it is a monster. **Jealousy** shows **disrespect**—**disrespect** for your wife and for yourself. If you really **respect** yourself and your wife, you will not be **jealous.** Why let **jealousy** hurt your marriage?

Also read this paragraph, and notice the meaning of each new word.

I **regard** you as one of my best friends. I **admire** your enthusiasm for life. I **respect** the fact that you take time to listen to other people's ideas, even if you do not always agree with them. You **honor** me by being my friend.

Write three sentences about each of the following stories. Use some of the new words from this unit. You may also use words from past units.

a. Mark watched David pick up the trophy. Mark felt that he should have the trophy, not David. David won everything in high school. Mark always came in second or third. That was true in sports, in studies, even in dating.

1. _____

_____

_____

regard (n)	
admire (v)	
disrespect (n)	
respect (v, n)	
worship (v)	
resent (v)	
jealousy (n)	
honor (v, n)	
disregard (v, n)	
jealous (adj)	

2. _____

_____

_____

3. _____

_____

_____

b. There are many ways to show how much you think of a person. You can tell the person. You can try to do something special for the person. Sometimes the person doesn't know how much you value him or her.

1. _____

_____

_____

2. _____

_____

_____

3. _____

_____

_____

c. The Heisman Trophy is given each year to the best college football player.

1. _____

_____

_____

regard (n)

admire (v)

disrespect (n)

respect (v, n)

worship (v)

resent (v)

jealousy (n)

honor (v, n)

disregard (v, n)

jealous (adj)

Write your own paragraph or story (five to seven sentences) using **five** or more of the new words you have learned.

2. _____

_____

_____

3. _____

_____

_____

_____

_____

_____

_____

_____

_____

_____

_____

_____

Using the New Words   Look at the **new** word in each sentence. Change the **new** word to the correct part of speech to fill in the blank.

Example: Ron Guidry pitches for the New York Yankees. He is a

_____.

You answer: pitcher

1. A man who shows **bravery** is a _____ man.

2. **Jealousy** can cause problems in a marriage. Married people should

try not to be _____.

3. The man was convicted of **arson**. The _____ will go to prison.

4. That soldier was a **coward**. His _____ actions helped the enemy.

5. It is a **delight** to have Sue as a guest. She is a _____ guest.

6. Wesley **accused** Rhett of stealing his girlfriend. The

_____ was true.

7. She did a **shameful** thing. She should be _____ of herself.

8. I feel no **guilt**. I am not _____.

9. It was a **pleasure** to walk through the garden. It was a

_____ walk.

10. Angela is **enthusiastic** about racketball. She shows her

_____ by playing every day.

Suffixes, Prefixes, and Roots

Match each prefix with its meaning.

_____ 1. ad-   a. again

_____ 2. re-   b. take away

_____ 3. dis-   c. into

_____ 4. in-   d. to

Identify the part of speech of each of these words. Write **n** (noun), **v** (verb), **adj** (adjective), or **adv** (adverb) in the blank next to the word.

_____ 1. envious

_____ 2. laughable

_____ 3. purist

_____ 4. amazement

_____ 5. helpful

_____ 6. arrangement

_____ 7. artistic

_____ 8. tremendous

_____ 9. senseless

_____ 10. happiness

Using the Related Words

Underline the word which correctly completes each sentence.

1. The children danced _____.
   delight   delightful   delightfully

2. The movie will _____ most audiences.
   please   pleasure   pleasant   pleasantly

3. The child _____ ignored his mother.

   shame   ashamed   shameful   shamefully

4. Teenagers often _____ movie stars.

   admire   admiration   admiring   admiringly

5. Children should not be _____ to their parents.

   disrespect   disrespectful   disrespectfully

6. Gunther Gabel Williams _____ walks into the
   lions' cage every day.

   bold   boldly   bolder

7. Kim was _____ surprised when she failed the
   test.

   displease   unpleasant   unpleasantly   displeasure

8. We _____ awaited the results of the Miss America
   contest.

   eager   eagerly   eagerness

9. The young girl _____ walked up to the large dog.

   fear   fearless   fearlessly   fearlessness

10. The _____ man supported his children after his
    divorce.

    honor   honorable   honorably

Getting the Right Idea   Read these sentences carefully. Complete the sentences which follow by
writing the correct person or thing (noun) in each blank.

1. Philip is a judge. Dale respects him.

   _____ is respectful.

   _____ is respectable.

2. Randy feels bad for stealing.

_____ is ashamed.

_____ is shameful.

3. Lou committed a crime by starting a fire.

Arson is a _____.

_____ is an arsonist.

4. Frank stole a pencil. Mariana said Tim did it.

_____ was blamed.

_____ was at fault.

5. Terry is afraid of everything. Mark is afraid of nothing.

_____ is fearless.

_____ is fearful.

Writing a Paragraph   Write a paragraph using five or more of these words.

blame	enjoy	bravery
blaze	jealous	ignite
fearless	pleasure	ashamed

_____

_____

_____

_____

_____

_____

_____

Synonyms

Match each word in column A with its synonym in column B. A synonym is a word that means the same or almost the same and that is the same part of speech. (10 points)

Example: bravery (n)   John's **bravery** surprised all his friends.

You choose: fearlessness (n)   John's **fearlessness** surprised all his friends.

A

_____ 1. guilty

_____ 2. pleasure

_____ 3. enthusiasm

_____ 4. delightful

_____ 5. accuse

_____ 6. boldness

_____ 7. scorch

_____ 8. honor

_____ 9. ignite

_____ 10. shame

B

a. blame

b. courage

c. at fault

d. burn

e. enjoyment

f. resent

g. eagerness

h. set on fire

i. guilt

j. pleasant

k. respect

Antonyms

Match each word in column A with its antonym in column B. An antonym is a word that means the opposite or nearly the opposite and that is the same part of speech. (10 points)

Example: good (adj)　Harry's work is very **good**.

You choose: bad (adj)　Harry's work is very **bad**.

A

_____ 1. pleasurable

_____ 2. eager

_____ 3. fearlessness

_____ 4. blameless

_____ 5. unpleasant

_____ 6. bold

_____ 7. ashamed

_____ 8. enjoy

_____ 9. admiration

_____ 10. shameful

B

a. honorable

b. unenjoyable

c. hate

d. proud

e. cowardice

f. delightful

g. scorch

h. cowardly

i. guilty

j. disrespect

k. unenthusiastic

Parts of Speech

You may not know the meanings of these words, but you have learned some prefixes (word-beginnings) and suffixes (word-endings). Therefore, you can tell whether these words are adjectives, verbs, nouns, or adverbs. Write **adj** for adjective, **v** for verb, **n** for noun, or **adv** for adverb. (10 points)

_____ 1. pessimistic

_____ 2. bravely

_____ 3. tremendous

_____ 4. homeless

_____ 5. homelessness

_____ 6. rainy

_____ 7. pianist

_____ 8. reliable

_____ 9. hopeful

_____ 10. education

The Right Word   Circle the word which best fits each sentence. (20 points)

1. I love to bowl. I think bowling is _____.

   eager   enjoyable   enthusiastic   enjoyment

2. He started a fire with a match. He used a match to _____ the fire.

   inflame   scorch   ignite   blaze

3. Stanley did a terrible thing. His action was _____.

   ashamed   guilt   guilty   shameful

4. Glen never worries about being hurt. He is a _____ person.

   brave   bravery   courage   boldness

5. I wish I could draw as well as Hazel. I _____ her artistic ability.

   regard   jealous   admire   disregard

6. Someone broke my bicycle. I wonder who is _____.

   guilt   fault   at fault   shame

7. Loretta studies very hard. She is _____ to make good grades.

   admire   regard   enthusiasm   eager

8. Gasoline burns very easily. It is very _____.

   blaze   flare   flammable   ignite

9. Dorothy always lies and cheats. We cannot _____ a person like her.

   respect   regard   resent   remind

10. Carl was careless with his cigarette. It fell out of his hand and
    _____ his wife's favorite table.

   blazed   scorched   inflamed   glowed

Sentences

Write one sentence of your own for each word. Be sure your sentences show the difference between the words in each pair. (40 points)

Example: careful   Laura is a **careful** person.

           carefully   Laura works very **carefully**.

1. enthusiasm _____

    enthusiastic _____

2. shame _____

    shameful _____

3. jealous _____

    jealousy _____

4. disrespect _____

    disrespectful _____

5. cowardly _____

    cowardice _____

6. guilt _____

    guilty _____

7. inflame _____

    flammable _____

8. fault _____

    at fault _____

9. flare _____

    glow _____

10. worship _____

    admire _____

Paragraphs

For each set of words below write a short paragraph using the words given. You may use the words in any order. In each paragraph include five or more sentences. (10 points)

1. blaze   flame   arson   accuse   ignite

_____

_____

_____

_____

_____

_____

_____

2. enjoy   pleasure   eager   fearless   courage

_____

_____

_____

_____

_____

_____

_____

words to learn

unit 6

remember	remind
memory	reminder
memorize	memorial
recall	memorandum
relive	memo

unit 7

accept	rejection
acceptance	permit
refuse	permission
refusal	allow
reject	decline

unit 8

view	glance
stare	glare
gaze	visit
watch	sightseeing
observe	inspect

unit 9

advice	scold
advise	punish
advisor	persuade
reward	encourage
praise	encouragement

unit 10

injure	ruin
damage	construct
destroy	construction
destruction	establish
disaster	establishment

units 6-10 pretest

Matching

Match each word with a word that means the same or almost the same. Make sure that the words are the same part of speech (noun, verb, adjective, adverb).

Unit
Key

(7)	_____	1. refuse	a.	hurt
(8)	_____	2. gaze	b.	build
(10)	_____	3. injure	c.	a terrible event
(10)	_____	4. ruin	d.	look quickly at
(7)	_____	5. refusal	e.	rejection
(10)	_____	6. disaster	f.	establish
(10)	_____	7. construct	g.	decline
(8)	_____	8. glance	h.	opinion
(9)	_____	9. advice	i.	stare
(9)	_____	10. encourage	j.	destroy
			k.	urge

Fill in the Blank

Write the best word from this list in each blank below.

reward   scold   praise   punish

**Unit
Key**

(9) 1. To say something good about someone is to

_____ him.

(9) 2. To tell people that they have done something bad is to

_____ them.

(9) 3. To give someone something for a good action is to

_____ him.

(9) 4. To take away something from someone for a bad action is to

_____ him.

Sentences

Write one sentence of your own for each word here.

**Unit
Key**

(6)   1. remind _____

_____

(6)   2. recall _____

_____

(7)   3. permission _____

_____

(7)   4. allow _____

_____

(8)   5. sightseeing _____

_____

(6)   6. remember _____

_____

(8)   7. glare _____

_____

(9)   8. advise _____

_____

(9)   9. persuade _____

_____

(10) 10. establish _____

_____

Teacher's Comments:

Units to be Done: 6   7   8   9   10

unit 6

words to learn

remember	remind
memory	reminder
memorize	memorial
recall	memorandum
relive	memo

Definitions and Examples

remember*
(v)

To remember is to bring back to your mind; to keep in your mind; not to forget.

Example: Can you **remember** when you first saw snow?

Example: **Remember** to bring your books with you.

memory
(n)

Memory is the power or ability of remembering; **memory** is also what you remember.

Example: I have a good **memory** for names. But this course will improve my **memory** even more.

Example: **I have few memories** of my grandfather, but I do have a very early **memory** of my grandmother holding my hand at the zoo.

memorize
(v)

To **memorize** is to make something a part (a permanent part) of your memory; to learn by heart.

Example: Try to **memorize** every prefix (word-beginning) on the list.

recall
(v)

To **recall** is to remember; "to call back" to your mind.

Example: Can you **recall** what he said to you before he ran out?

relive
(v)

To **relive** is to experience again a past event. (Often that "living again" is only in your imagination.)

Example: I wish I could **relive** my high school days.

Example: Sometimes my grandmother sits on the front porch in her rocking chair. She sings to herself. I know she is **reliving** her childhood.

Fill in each blank with one of these words.

remember	recall	memorize
memory	relive	

1. Schoolchildren have to _____ the Pledge of Allegiance to the flag.

2. Many people find it hard to _____ the names of people they meet.

3. Old people often remember their childhood. Sometimes they

   wish they could _____ their early years.

4. My grandmother has a pleasant _____ of her life in Ireland.

5. Can you _____ her address?

---

remind*
(v)

To **remind** is to bring back to someone's mind; to help someone remember.

Example: That boy **reminds** Ann of her brother.

Example: Can you **remind** me to bring my books?

reminder
(n)

A **reminder** is something that helps you to remember something.

Example: The Lincoln Memorial is a **reminder** of our sixteenth president.

memorial
(n)

A **memorial** is a reminder of a great event or person; sometimes it is a place.

Example: Have you visited the Jefferson **Memorial**?

memorandum
(n)

A **memorandum** is a note to help one remember something; a reminder.

Example: We received the **memorandum** from the dean's office on Monday.

memo
(n)

Memo is the short form of the word **memorandum**.

Example: I sent two **memos** to the president about this situation.

∗To use these words correctly, you must know this pattern.

remind + (someone) + of + (something)

Examples: James reminded Albert **of** his appointment.
Denise reminded me **of** what I had to do.

When we use a "that-clause" after the object, we do not use **of**.

Example: Ramon reminded his mother **that** she had to go.

We cannot use **remember** in the pattern given above. We *cannot* say:

James remembered Albert of his appointment.
Denise remembered me of what I had to do.
Ramon remembered his mother that she had to go.

Fill in each blank with one of these words.

remind
reminder

memorandum
memo

memorial

1. The secretary sent a _____ to each member of the committee.

2. The Martin Luther King Library in Washington is a

_____ to Dr. Martin Luther King, Jr.

3. Please _____ Arthur to meet me in the cafeteria.

4. A picture of a fat person is posted on my refrigerator as a

_____ not to eat too much.

5. The dean sent out a memo, or _____, telling faculty members how they could make up the snow days.

Word-Roots, Word-Beginnings (Prefixes), and Word-Endings (Suffixes)

1. An important root for this unit is **-mem-**. **Mem** means **remember**—an easy root to **remember** or to **memorize** or to keep in your **memory**.

2. You can see the prefix **re-** which means **back** or **again**.

recall   re + call means to **remember** or to **call back**.

relive   re + live means to **live again**.

3. You can also see two word-endings (suffixes): **-er** and **-ize**.

reminder   remind (v) + **er** means **that which reminds**. (**-er** makes a noun.)

memorize   memory + **ize** means to **make part of your memory**. (**-ize** makes a verb.)

Related Words

commemorate (v)	memorize (v)	recall (v)
commemoration (n)	memory (n)	recollection (n)
	memorable (adj)	

Using These Words

Circle the correct word for each pair.

remember (v)

recall (v)

reminder (n)

memory (n)

relive (v)

memorial (n)

memo (n)

memorize (v)

remind (v)

memorandum (n)

1. I often (remember/remind) my first trip to Washington and a tour I took to the Lincoln (Memory/Memorial). The sad, giant statue of Lincoln almost took my breath away. It (reminded/recalled) me of a statue I had seen of Moses. I enjoy history. In high school I (relived/memorized) some of the words from Lincoln's Gettysburg Address. I (reminder/recalled) those words as I stood there.

2. Mr. Frost was afraid that his lawyer, Ms. Rivers, might forget their appointment. He asked his secretary to send a (memo/memory) to Ms. Rivers. The (memorandum/remind) gave the time, place, and reason for the meeting.

3. I have many pleasant (memories/memos) of my first year in college. I (remind/remember) how I felt being away from home. And I (remind/recall) the long hours I had to study. But still, if I could (relive/remember) those days, I would.

Read this example of a memo. Notice how the new words are used.

MEMORANDUM

TO: Adam and Eve

FROM: God

SUBJECT: First Things

1. Please **memorize** all the names of the animals, trees, plants, and fruits by the end of this week. (This will prevent misunderstanding later.)

2. The sign on the Forbidden Tree, "Do not eat this fruit," is meant as a **reminder** of what we talked about. Do not put signs on any of the other trees.

3. Do not come to me with your arguments. As you may **recall**, Adam, you were the one who didn't want to be alone.

4. **Remind** me to talk with you both about my idea for the seventh day of the week—Sunday, I think you call it. (Sun day, you have a nice way with words.) As I see it, it could be a **memorial** to creation, a day of rest, relaxation. You could have picnics, go sightseeing, hold Super Bowls.

Now read this story to see how other words in this lesson can be used.

Jeff gazed at the painting over his desk. Karen had done it for him just before he left her in August to return to college. When he looked at it, many things came to mind.

We can write the following sentences to continue this story:

Jeff wished he could **relive** those days with Karen.

He **remembered** the first time they met.

He **recalled** that she had asked him to go out. What a switch!

remember (v)

recall (v)

reminder (n)

memory (n)

relive (v)

memorial (n)

memo (n)

memorize (v)

remind (v)

memorandum (n)

Write three sentences about each of the following stories. Use some of the new words from this unit. You may also use words from past units.

a. My grandfather is 73. He lives in a small apartment now in the middle of Los Angeles, but in his mind he lives on a large wheat farm in Kansas. In his mind he is a boy again.

1. _____

_____

_____

2. _____

_____

_____

3. _____

_____

_____

remember (v)

recall (v)

reminder (n)

memory (n)

relive (v)

memorial (n)

memo (n)

memorize (v)

remind (v)

memorandum (n)

b. I have a poor head for dates, especially birthdays. So I am always trying to find a way to make sure I don't forget friends' and relatives' birthdays.

1. _____

_____

_____

2. _____

_____

_____

3. _____

_____

_____

Write your own paragraph, memo, or story (five to seven sentences) using **five** or more of the new words you have learned. Use any of the paragraphs in this unit as an example.

_____

_____

_____

_____

_____

_____

_____

_____

_____

_____

unit 7

words to learn

accept	rejection
acceptance	permit
refuse	permission
refusal	allow
reject	decline

Definitions and Examples

accept
(v)

To **accept** means to take what someone gives you.

Example: A friend gives you a gift. You take it and say, "Thank you." You **accepted** your friend's gift.

acceptance
(n)

Acceptance means the action of accepting, the action of taking what someone gives you.

Example: When you said, "Thank you," you showed your **acceptance** of your friend's gift.

decline
(v)

To **decline** means not to accept, but to be polite about it.

Example: A friend gives you a gift. You do not take (accept) it. You say, "No, thank you." You **declined** your friend's gift.

refuse
(v)

To **refuse** means to say, "I won't."

Example: Someone asks you to leave the room. You say, "No, I won't leave the room." You **refuse** to leave the room.

To **refuse** also means to say, "I won't accept"; to decline strongly.

Example: You help your friend fix his car. He wants to pay you. You do not want to take (accept) his money. You say to him, "I won't accept your money." You **refuse** your friend's money.

refusal
(n)

Refusal means the action of refusing.

Example: When you said, "No, I won't leave the room," you showed your **refusal** to leave.

Example: When you told your friend, "I won't accept your money," you showed your **refusal** of his money.

reject
(v)

To **reject** means to say, "I don't want it; you keep it."

Example: You have a problem. Your friend says, "I will help you." You say, "I don't want your help." You **reject** your friend's help.

rejection
(n)

Rejection means the action of rejecting.

Example: When you said, "I don't want your help," you showed your **rejection** of your friend's help.

permit*
(v)
allow*
(v)

To **permit** and to **allow** both mean to say, "Yes, you may."

Example: Wayne asks you, "May I use your car today?" You say, "Yes, you may use my car today." You **permit (allow)** Wayne to use your car.

permission
(n)

Permission is the action of permitting, the action of saying, "Yes, you may."

Example: When you said to Wayne, "Yes, you may use my car today," you gave Wayne **permission** to use your car.

---

*To use these words correctly, you must know these patterns.

permit + (someone) + to + verb

allow + (someone) + to +verb

Examples: Jorge always permits Karla **to** use his car.
Jorge always allows Karla **to** use his car.

Let means the same as **permit** and **allow.** We do not use **to** with the verb **let.** With **let** we must use this pattern:

let + (someone) + verb

Example: Jorge always **lets** Karla **use** his car.

Fill in each blank with one of these words.

accept	refusal	permit
acceptance	reject	allow
decline	rejection	permission
refuse		

1. Karen has the dean's _____ to miss class this week.

2. Chun offered Fred $1,000 for his car. Fred decided to

   _____ Chun's money and sold him the car.

3. Does your math teacher _____ cuts in that class?

4. Betty was invited to Juanita's birthday party. She could not go, so

   she had to _____ the invitation.

5. Kent wanted to get into a fraternity. Sigma Phi's

   _____ of him made him happy.

6. The baby will _____ to eat his food. He will throw it all on the floor.

7. The government's _____ to control gas prices means we will pay more and more to fill our gas tanks.

Word-Roots, Word-Beginnings (Prefixes), and Word-Endings (Suffixes)

Look at these words. See how the endings make new words.

refusal — refuse + **al** means **action of refusing. (-al** makes a noun here. Usually it makes an adjective.)

acceptance — accept + **ance** means **action of accepting.** (-ance makes a noun.)

rejection — reject + **ion** means **action of rejecting. (-ion** makes a noun.)

permission — permit + **tion** means **action of permitting. (-tion** makes a noun. *Notice:* **tt** becomes **ss.**)

The root **-ject-** is very important. It means **throw.** To **reject** means to **throw back.** If you offer me something, and I **reject** your offer, I "throw it back to you" *or* I refuse to accept it. With other word-beginnings the root **-ject-** gives us:

inject	in + **ject** means to **throw into** (to give medicine to somebody with a needle).
eject	e + **ject** means to **throw out** (to make someone leave a place).

Related Words

inject (v)	eject (v)	accept (v)
injection (n)	ejection (n)	acceptance (n)
		acceptable (adj)

Using These Words
Circle the correct word in each pair.

accept (v)

refuse (v)

rejection (n)

acceptance (n)

refusal (n)

permit (v)

permission (n)

decline (v)

reject (v)

allow (v)

Yesterday my car was broken. I had to go out of town. I asked my friend,

"Will you (permission/permit) me to use your car?" My friend said, "Yes, I

will (reject/allow) you to use it." When I came back, I wanted to give him

some money because he (allowed/rejected) me to use his car. However,

he (refused/accepted) it. I invited him to go out for dinner, but he

(declined/accepted) my invitation. I cannot understand why he

(rejected/rejection) both my attempts to repay him. A few days later I

bought him a gift, and he took it and said, "Thank you." His

(acceptance/permission) really surprised me because I expected another

(reject/rejection).

Read this story.

David stopped on the way home from work to cash his paycheck. However, the teller at the bank would not cash it because David did not have an account at that bank. David showed the teller his driver's license and two credit cards, but the teller said that the bank still could not cash the check. David became angry. The teller said that David could talk to the manager, but David said that he didn't want to do that.

We can write these sentences about this story:

The teller **refused** to cash David's paycheck.

The teller would not **allow** David to cash his check.

The teller would not **accept** David's identification.

David was very angry because the teller would not **permit** him to cash his check.

The teller's **refusal** to cash David's check made him angry.

David **declined** to talk to the manager.

David **refused** to talk to the manager.

Write three sentences about each of the following stories. Use some of the words from this unit. You may also use words from past units.

accept (v)

refuse (v)

rejection (n)

acceptance (n)

refusal (n)

permit (v)

permission (n)

decline (v)

reject (v)

allow (v)

a. Melvin wants to become a lawyer. He applied to a law school several months ago. Today he learned that the law school did not take him.

1. _____

_____

_____

2. _____

_____

_____

3. _____

_____

_____

b. Arturo wants to be on the varsity football team. He tried out this fall. The coach gave him a position on the team.

1. _____

_____

_____

2. _____

_____

_____

3. _____

_____

_____

accept (v)
refuse (v)
rejection (n)
acceptance (n)
refusal (n)
permit (v)
permission (n)
decline (v)
reject (v)
allow (v)

c. Craig bought an engagement ring for Pamela, but Pamela did not want to marry Craig. She did not take his ring.

1. _____

_____

_____

2. _____

_____

_____

3. _____

_____

_____

d. Mrs. Hefler was not feeling well. The doctor told her to go on a diet. He told her, "You may not eat cake or candy." Mrs. Hefler did not obey her doctor.

1. _____

_____

_____

2. _____

_____

_____

3. _____

_____

_____

accept (v)

refuse (v)

rejection (n)

acceptance (n)

refusal (n)

permit (v)

permission (n)

decline (v)

reject (v)

allow (v)

e. Patrick wanted to join the army. The army doctor examined Patrick and said, "You may not join the army." The army did not take him.

1. _____

_____

_____

2. _____

_____

_____

3. _____

_____

_____

Write your own paragraph (five to seven sentences). Use **five** or more of the new words you have learned. Use any of the paragraphs in this unit as an example.

_____

_____

_____

_____

_____

_____

_____

_____

_____

_____

unit 8

words to learn	view	sightseeing
	watch	glance
	observe	glare
	inspect	stare
	visit	gaze

Definitions and Examples

view
(n)

A **view** is what you see; a scene.

Example: I have a beautiful **view** of the Library of Congress from my window.

watch*
(v)

To **watch** is to look at carefully; to guard; to protect.

Example: **Watch** how I do this. Then you try it.

Example. **Watch** my book while I'm gone.

observe*
(v)

To **observe** is to look at or notice.

Example: **I have observed** him in class, and I think he is a good worker.

inspect*
(v)

To **inspect** is to look at closely; to examine; to "look into."

Example: He **inspected** each boy's desk, locker, and room. But he still didn't find the missing key.

visit
(v, n)

To **visit** (v) is to go or come to see someone or something; to stay with as a guest.

Example: Tomorrow our class will **visit** the National Gallery of Art.

Example: Next summer we hope to **visit** friends in California.

A **visit** (n) is the act of visiting; a stay as a guest.

Example: Your family made my **visit** to San Francisco very enjoyable.

sightseeing
(n)

Sightseeing is seing places of interest, going on a tour; "seeing the sights" (often used with "to go").

Example: I would like to go **sightseeing** with you this afternoon, but I have a lot of homework to do.

Example: I enjoy **sightseeing.**

★With the verbs **watch, observe, inspect**, we do not use **at**; we use this pattern:

watch + (something or someone)

observe + (something or someone)

inspect + (something or someone)

Examples: I **watched television** last night.
The principal **observed** the biology **class.**
The mechanic **inspected** my **car.**

Fill in each blank with one of these words.

| view | observe | visit |
| watch | inspect | sightseeing |

1. On my way to work, I often _____ that many gas stations are closed.

2. On the Fourth of July many people _____ the fireworks.

3. The health department will _____ restaurants carefully.

4. When I am in New York, I always go _____ .

5. The _____ of the Rockies in spring is beautiful.

6. Tanya always wanted to _____ Austria.

glance* (v,n)	To **glance** (v) is to look quickly, to look for a moment. *Example:* She **glanced** at the list of words before she went into class. *Example:* He **glanced** at her out of the corner of his eye. A **glance** (n) is a short, quick look. (See the word "lance" inside the word "glance." Think of a lance, a spear point coming out from your eye. That's what a glance is—a quick, sharp look.) *Example:* He didn't give his ex-girlfriend a **glance** all evening.
glare* (v)	To **glare** is to look with anger at something or someone. *Example:* She **glared** at him when he said he thought her friend was cute. *Example:* Don't **glare** at me when I tell you to get to work.
stare* (v, n)	To **stare** (v) is to look at someone or something for a long time. *Example:* The whole class **stared** at Professor Ludens when he told them no one had passed the test. A **stare** (n) is a long, strong look; the act of staring. *Example:* His **stare** made me uncomfortable.
gaze* (v)	To **gaze** is to look for a long time at something or someone and to be dreaming while you are looking. *Example:* He **gazed** out the window at the leaves changing color and thought of home and Thanksgiving.

*To use these words correctly you must know this pattern.

stare + at + (something or someone)

gaze + at + (something or someone)

glance + at + (something or someone)

glare + at + (something or someone)

Examples: John stared **at** his paper.
Martha gazed **at** the statue.
I glanced **at** my watch.
The student glared **at** the teacher.

The verb **look** follows this same pattern:

Pedro looked **at** his paper.

Fill in each blank with one of these words.

glance   stare
glare   gaze

1. Tonight Sharon will _____ dreamily at the moonlight on the water as the boat slowly moves along the river.

2. People always _____ at a performer on a tightrope.

3. Sometimes basketball players _____ quickly at the crowd and then shoot the ball through the hoop.

4. Everyday the two boys _____ at each other. They are waiting for school to let out so they can fight each other.

Word-Roots, Word-Beginnings (Prefixes), and Word-Endings (Suffixes)

1. We have two interesting roots in this unit: **-spect-** (**-spec-**) and **-vis-**.

-Spect- means to **look at**; to **watch**; to **observe**.

-Vis- means to **see**.

There are many interesting English words you can understand with these roots:

spectator - one who looks at
spectacle - something one looks at
vision - something seen or the ability to see
visible - can be seen
visitor - one who visits (or sees)

2. You can see one prefix (word-beginning) in this unit: **in-**. Here it means **into**. When you combine it with the root **-spect-** in the word **inspect**, it means to **look into very closely**.

3. You can see several suffixes (word-endings) in the related words.

    a. **-tion** makes a noun meaning **the act of**. So **inspect** with the suffix **-tion** becomes **inspection** meaning **the act of inspecting**.

    b. **-er** or **-or** makes a noun meaning **a person who**. So **inspect** with the suffix **-or** becomes **inspector** meaning **a person who inspects**.

4. The word **sightseeing** is made from two words, **sight** and **see**. When you put them together, you get a new word. This kind of word is called a compound word. You see many of them in English.

Notice how the word **watch** in this unit makes some compound words:

watch + man makes watchman
watch + dog makes watchdog
watch + tower makes watchtower

Related Words	inspect (v)	observe (v)	
	inspection (n)	observation (n)	spectator (n)
	inspector (n)	observer (n)	spectacle (n)
			spectacular (adj)
	visit (v)	view (v)	
	visit (n)	view (n)	sightseeing (n)
	visitor (n)	viewer (n)	sightseer (n)
	vision (n)		
	visible (adj)		

Using These Words
Circle the correct word in each pair.

view (n)

watch (v)

glance (v, n)

stare (v, n)

observe (v)

glare (v)

sightseeing (n)

gaze (v)

inspect (v)

visit (v, n)

1. It is interesting to (watch/glance) tourists in Washington, D.C. They (inspect/stare) wide-eyed at the Lincoln Memorial and the Washington Monument. They are the ones who hang their heads out of car windows. They have come to D.C. for (sightseeing/stare), and they are going to (gaze/visit) as many sights as they can on their trip.

2. Jim turned his head and (watched/glanced) at Mike's test paper. He hoped the teacher hadn't (observed/watched) him. If he could just get a quick (stare/glance) at Mike's paper, maybe Jim could pass the exam. But Mike (observed/stared) him and (inspected/glared) back at Jim. His look said, "(Watch/Stare) yourself! Be careful!"

Read this story.

I have always wanted to take a trip to San Francisco. Next week I plan to go there. I want to take a tour around the city. I hope I can stay there for a few days because you cannot see everything in one day. I especially want to see the Pacific Ocean. I will probably also see the Golden Gate Bridge because one of my dreams has always been to look at the sun setting behind that famous bridge.

We can write these sentences about this story:

I have always wanted to **visit** San Francisco.

I want to go **sightseeing** around the city.

I want to **gaze** at the Pacific Ocean.

I will **stare** at the ocean.

I want to **watch** the sun set behind the Golden Gate Bridge.

Write three sentences about each of the following stories. Use some of the new words from this unit. You may also use words from past units.

a. It is not not polite to look at people when they are eating. Looking at people when they are eating makes them nervous. Sometimes they give you an angry look.

1. _____

_____

_____

view (n)

watch (v)

glance (v, n)

stare (v, n)

observe (v)

glare (v)

sightseeing (n)

gaze (v)

inspect (v)

visit (v, n)

2. _____

_____

_____

3. _____

_____

b. I went to see a friend in the hospital. When I walked into the room, he was looking out the window.

1. _____

_____

_____

2. _____

_____

_____

3. _____

_____

_____

c. I can see the lake from my apartment window. I like to look at the children ice skating during the winter. Sometimes when I look out of my window, I wish I could be a child again.

1. _____

_____

_____

view (n)

watch (v)

glance (v, n)

stare (v, n)

observe (v)

glare (v)

sightseeing (n)

gaze (v)

inspect (v)

visit (v, n)

2. _____

_____

_____

3. _____

_____

_____

d. The manager looked closely at the list of names in front of her. She wasn't sure who would work on Saturday. A quick look at the last name gave her the answer. Kay would be eager to work. The manager would ask her.

1. _____

_____

_____

2. _____

_____

_____

3. _____

_____

_____

Write one story or paragraph (five to seven sentences) using **five** or more of the words you have learned.

view (n)

watch (v)

glance (v, n)

stare (v, n)

observe (v)

glare (v)

sightseeing (n)

gaze (v)

inspect (v)

visit (v, n)

unit 9

advice	encouragement
advise	praise
advisor	reward
persuade	scold
encourage	punish

Definitions and Examples

advice
(n)

Advice is an opinion or helpful information you tell to someone.

Example: My doctor's **advice** was that I should stop smoking.

advise
(v)

To **advise** is to give an opinion or helpful information to someone.

Example: The teacher **advised** Fred to drop the course he was failing.

advisor
(n)

An **advisor** is a person who gives another person an opinion or helpful information.

Example: My **advisor** thinks I should major in history.

persuade
(v)

To **persuade** means to make someone believe something or do something which he or she **doesn't** want to do; to change one's mind.

Example: Sue wanted to go to Yale, but her mother **persuaded** her to go to Harvard. Sue went to Harvard.

encourage
(v)

To **encourage** means to urge someone to do well or try hard.

Example: Nancy wanted to go to Duke University, and her teacher **encouraged** her to take the entrance exam.

encouragement
(n)

Encouragement is something which helps one to do better.

Example: Helen Keller's success is an **encouragement** to many handicapped people.

Example: I got a lot of support and **encouragement** from my parents when I decided to go to college.

Fill in each blank with one of these words.

advice	advisor	encourage
advise	persuade	encouragement

1. Each student in college has a faculty _____ who helps her or him select courses.

2. Dave tried to _____ Henry to stop studying and go to the movies. Henry went to the movies with Dave.

3. The fans' cheers _____ the team to try harder.

4. Doctors _____ people to stop smoking.

5. Paul's boss gave him some helpful _____ about his budget.

6. A baby just learning to walk gets a lot of _____.

---

praise
(v, n)

To **praise** (v) means to say something good about something or someone.

Example: Romeo **praised** Juliet's beauty.

Praise (n) is saying that something or someone is good.

Example: Pat worked hard to win her father's **praise.**

reward
(v, n)

To **reward** (v) is to give someone something for a good action.

Example: They **rewarded** the girl for saving the drowning boy.

A **reward** (n) is a prize you give to someone for doing something good.

Example: They gave the girl a large **reward** for returning their lost dog.

scold (v)	To **scold** means to tell someone that he has been bad or has done something bad. Usually you **scold** only someone smaller, weaker, or less important than you are.
	Example: Linda **scolded** her little boy for making a mess in the room.
punish (v)	To **punish** means to hurt someone or take something away from someone because he has done something wrong.
	Example: Pete hit his brother. Pete's mother **punished** him by sending him to his room. He could not go out with his friends.

Fill in each blank with one of these words.

praise   scold
reward   punish

1. Dora returned the lost wallet and got a large _____.

2. Some people think it is a good idea to _____ children by spanking them.

3. The woman will _____ her daughter loudly for running into the street.

4. The guides _____ the Mona Lisa as they proudly show it to the visitors.

Word-Roots, Word-Beginnings (Prefixes), and Word-Endings (Suffixes)

Look at these words. See how the endings or beginnings make new words.

advisor	advise + **or** means **one who advises.**
encouragement	encourage + **ment** means **the thing which encourages.** (-ment makes a noun.)
encourage	en + courage means to **put courage into.** If you put courage into people, you help them believe they can succeed. The root of **courage** is discussed in Unit 3.

Related Words

punish (v)	persuade (v)	discourage (v)
punishment (n)	persuasion (n)	discouragement (n)
	persuasive (adj)	discouraging (adj)
	persuasively (adv)	discouragingly (adv)

encourage (v)	scold (v)
encouragement (n)	scolding (n)
encouraging (adj)	
encouragingly (adv)	

Using These Words

Circle the correct word in each pair.

advice (n)

praise (v, n)

punish (v)

advise (v)

reward (v, n)

persuade (v)

encouragement (n)

advisor (n)

scold (v)

encourage (v)

1. Sharon's teachers thought she should go to college. They gave her a lot of (encourage/encouragement) because she was a good student. They (praised/encouraged) her to take the college entrance exam. Because of their (advice/advise) she tried it. She passed!

2. My dog Benji does not like me to speak angrily to him. He hangs his head when I (scold/praise) him. I yell at him for many things, but I get really angry only when he knocks over the garbage can. Then I (punish/reward) him by locking him in the basement. When he is good, I (praise/advise) him by telling him he is a good dog. Sometimes I give him a dog bone to (reward/scold) him for being so good.

Read this story.

This was Kate's first semester at college. She was homesick and worried about her work. She didn't know what to do. She was afraid of failing. She needed to talk to someone.

We can write the following sentences to continue this story:

Kate asked her roommate for **advice.**

Then she went to see her **advisor.**

Her advisor **persuaded** her to stay for the full semester.

He **advised** her to talk to her teachers.

Kate's math teacher, Miss Sims, **praised** her work in her course.

Kate was **encouraged** by her praise.

This **encouragement** made her work more in math.

Kate learned a lot in that course, and the teacher **rewarded** her with an "A."

Write four sentences about each of the following stories. Use some of the new words from this unit. You may also use words from past units.

advice (n)

praise (v, n)

punish (v)

advise (v)

reward (v, n)

persuade (v)

encouragement (n)

advisor (n)

scold (v)

encourage (v)

a. Becky is two years old. She likes to play with blocks. Her mother likes her to put away her blocks when she finishes playing. She doesn't like Becky to leave her blocks on the floor. When Becky picks up all her things, her mother tells her she is a good girl. Sometimes she gives her a lollipop for being so good. But when Becky leaves her blocks on the floor, her mother calls her a bad, bad girl.

1. _____

_____

_____

2. _____

_____

_____

3. _____

_____

_____

4. _____

_____

_____

b. Sidney doesn't know which foreign language he should take. Robby told him that he should take French. His science teacher told him to take German. The teacher who filled out his schedule told him that Spanish was the easiest language. He wanted Sidney to take Spanish so he would get a good grade. A letter from home helped Sidney decide. It said his family was moving to Italy. Sidney decided to take Italian.

1. _____

_____

_____

advice (n)

praise (v, n)

punish (v)

advise (v)

reward (v, n)

persuade (v)

encouragement (n)

advisor (n)

scold (v)

encourage (v)

Write your own paragraph (five to seven sentences) using **five** or more of the new words you have learned. Use any of the paragraphs in this unit as an example.

2. _____

_____

_____

3. _____

_____

_____

4. _____

_____

_____

_____

_____

_____

_____

_____

_____

_____

_____

_____

_____

_____

unit 10

injure	ruin
damage	construct
destroy	construction
destruction	establish
disaster	establishment

Definitions and Examples

injure
(v)

To **injure** means to hurt.

Example: The bad boy **injured** the little dog.

damage
(v, n)

To **damage** (v) means to hurt, injure, or break something.

Example: The wind **damaged** the small boat.

Damage (n) is any injury or break.

Example: The storm caused a lot of **damage.**

destroy
(v)

To **destroy** means to damage completely or to break completely and make useless.

Example: The fire **destroyed** the house.

destruction
(n)

Destruction is complete damage. It means making something useless.

Example: The **destruction** of the old hotel left 20 people homeless.

disaster
(n)

A **disaster** is an event which causes destruction, damage, and suffering.

Example: The crash of the 747 was the worst airplane **disaster** ever.

ruin
(v)

To **ruin** something is to destroy it.

Example: The storm **ruined** our cabbage plants.

Fill in each blank with one of these words.

injure   destroy   disaster
damage   destruction   ruin

1. An atomic bomb can _____ a city completely.

2. Even a small accident can _____ your car.

3. War is a great _____ .

4. Maybe the athlete will _____ himself playing football. I hope that he does not twist his ankle.

5. If it rains tomorrow, it will _____ our picnic.

construct
(v)

To **construct** means to build.

Example: They **constructed** that house in two months.

construction
(n)

Construction is the action of building or putting parts together to make something.

Example: The **construction** of the new cafeteria took one year.

establish
(v)

To **establish** means to start an organization.

Example: A photography club was **established** in our school last year.

establishment
(n)

An **establishment** is a start.

Example: The **establishment** of Gallaudet College in Washington, D.C., helped deaf students.

Fill in each blank with one of these words.

construct	establish
construction	establishment

1. The army will _____ a bridge over the river.

2. The _____ of a drug policy helped to reduce the number of students using drugs.

3. Henry Ford was the first American to _____ an automobile company.

4. The _____ of the gymnasium took several years.

Word-Roots, Word-Beginnings (Prefixes), and Word-Endings (Suffixes)

-**Struct**- is an important root to know. -**Struct**- means to build or to put together. It combines with word-beginnings and endings to make many English words. Some of them are:

structure   in**struct**ion   con**struct**   de**struct**ion

Related Words

reconstruct (v)	re-establish (v)	construct (v)
reconstruction (n)	re-establishment (n)	construction (n)
		constructive (adj)

destroy (v)	injure (v)
destruction (n)	injury (n)
destructive (adj)	

Using These Words
Circle the correct word in each pair.

injure (v)

destruction (n)

construct (v)

damage (v, n)

disaster (n)

construction (n)

establishment (n)

destroy (v)

ruin (v)

establish (v)

There was a great (disaster/destroy) in Xenia, Ohio. The whole town was

(disaster/destroyed) by a tornado. The (destruction/construction)

covered four square miles. Crops and gardens were (ruined/established)

in another 12 square miles. The Red Cross (construction/established)

a first aid station. Many families immediately began to (injure/construct)

new houses. The (establish/construction) was paid for by their insurance.

The (establishment/construct) of a good insurance plan years ago

helped them very much. They were happy that so few people were

(disaster/injured) and that the (destroy/destruction) could be repaired.

Read this story to see how these words can be used.

War is a great **disaster.** It **injures** people, **ruins** the land, and **damages** cities. Sometimes it **destroys** important buildings. The **destruction** of a hospital is very sad. People have to **construct** a new building. Sometimes there is no money for the **construction** of a new building. Then, doctors may **establish** a hospital in a school or church. This **establishment** lets them continue to take care of the sick and injured people.

Now read this story.

Rain is necessary for a garden, but too much rain can injure young plants. After I planted my tomatoes last year, it rained for two weeks. I had to protect my plants.

We can write these sentences about this situation:

Too much rain can **damage** young plants.

It can **ruin** a garden.

A heavy rain can knock the plants down and **destroy** their blossoms.

I had to **construct** shelters for my plants.

The **construction** of the shelters took me one day.

But they saved my tomatoes from **destruction.**

Write five sentences about each of the following stories.

injure (v)
destruction (n)
construct (v)
damage (v, n)
disaster (n)
construction (n)
establishment (n)
destroy (v)
ruin (v)
establish (v)

a. The drought (lack of rain) in Virginia was awful last year. It killed many crops. It hurt many other crops. Some farmers built pipelines to bring water to their animals. Other farmers lost all their money and their farms, too. It was a bad year to be a farmer.

1. _____

_____

_____

2. _____

_____

_____

3. _____

_____

_____

4. _____

_____

_____

5. _____

_____

_____

b. A club called "Model Train Engineers" was started in 1950. It tells people how to build things for their model trains. It helps people with toy trains. Some people build whole cities with bridges and tunnels and everything. It is fun.

1. _____

_____

_____

injure (v)

destruction (n)

construct (v)

damage (v, n)

disaster (n)

construction (n)

establishment (n)

destroy (v)

ruin (v)

establish (v)

Write a paragraph (five to seven sentences) using **five** or more of the new words you have learned in this unit. You may also use words from previous units.

2. _____

_____

_____

3. _____

_____

_____

4. _____

_____

_____

5. _____

_____

_____

_____

_____

_____

_____

_____

_____

_____

_____

_____

Using the New Words   Look at the **new** word in each sentence. Change the **new** word to the correct part of speech to fill in the blank.

Example: Ron Guidry **pitches** for the New York Yankees. He is a

_____.

You answer: <u>pitcher</u>

1. Someone who has a good **memory** can _____ things easily.

2. A driving **permit** gives a person _____ to drive a car.

3. The color green **reminds** me of St. Patrick's Day. A shamrock is

another good _____ of it.

4. The man **accepted** our offer. His _____ pleased us.

5. Jan went to her **advisor** to get _____ about her courses.

6. Floods cause a lot of **destruction**. They can _____ whole towns.

7. The author got a **rejection** from the publisher. They

_____ books they do not want to publish.

8. The girl **refused** to work overtime. Her _____ angered her boss.

9. Parents should **encourage** children to do their best. Children need a

lot of _____.

10. The **construction** of that new building will take four years. They have

to _____ it slowly and carefully.

Suffixes, Prefixes, and Roots

You studied several roots in these lessons. Match each root with its meaning.

_____ 1. -vis-   a. remember

_____ 2. -struct-   b. throw

_____ 3. -ject-   c. see

_____ 4. -mem-   d. look at

_____ 5. -spect-   e. build

From your knowledge of the suffixes in these lessons, mark the part of speech of each word here. Write **n** (noun), **v** (verb), **adj** (adjective), or **adv** (adverb) in the blank next to the word.

_____ 1. refusal

_____ 2. allegiance

_____ 3. legalize

_____ 4. admission

_____ 5. royal

_____ 6. surveyor

_____ 7. realize

_____ 8. armament

Using the Related Words

Underline the word which correctly completes each sentence.

1. The salesclerk talked so _____ that we bought the car.

   persuasion   persuasive   persuasively   persuade

2. A car must pass _____ twice a year in Virginia.

   inspect   inspector   inspection

3. After he fell on the ice, the boy was kept in the hospital for
   _____ .

   observe   observation   observer

4. The new clerk worked hard to do an _____ job.

   accept   acceptance   acceptable

5. The new dollar will _____ Susan B. Anthony.

   commemorate   commemorative   commemoration

6. The team members felt bad when they lost the game. They were very
   _____ .

   ejected   injected   rejected   dejected

7. Did your friend _____ you to go on vacation with
   him?

   persuade   persuasion   persuasive   persuasively

8. Our old club fell apart. We want to _____ it.

   re-establish   re-establishment

9. Losing 20 games in a row will _____ any team.

   discourage   discouragement

10. We have a great _____ of the lake from our cabin.

    view   viewer

Getting the Right Idea   Read these sentences carefully. Complete the sentences which follow by
writing the correct person or thing (noun) in each blank.

1. Ed and Joe were walking on the road. A car stopped. The driver
   offered them a ride. Joe got in. Ed continued walking.

   _____ accepted a ride.

   _____ declined a ride.

2. Fran looked quickly at the woman's green hair. Ann continued to look at it until the woman was out of sight.

_____ stared at the hair.

_____ glanced at the hair.

3. Barry broke a glass. Clyde cleaned it up.

_____ should be scolded.

_____ should be praised.

4. The frost hurt the crops. The farmer got no oranges from his trees and only half as many lemons as he expected.

The _____ crop was ruined.

The _____ crop was damaged.

5. The boss wanted Dan and Earl to work late. Dan worked late. Earl did not.

The boss persuaded _____ to work late.

The boss encouraged _____ to work late.

Writing a Paragraph   Write a paragraph using five or more of these words.

remember   watch   advice
inspect   disaster   accept
damage   allow   persuade
remind

_____

_____

_____

_____

_____

_____

_____

_____

_____

Synonyms

Match each word in column A with its synonym in column B. A synonym is a word that means the same or almost the same and that is the same part of speech. (10 points)

Example: bravery (n)   John's **bravery** surprised all of his friends.

You choose: fearlessness (n)   John's **fearlessness** surprised all of his friends.

A

_____ 1. permit

_____ 2. watch

_____ 3. construct

_____ 4. encourage

_____ 5. memorize

_____ 6. refuse

_____ 7. damage

_____ 8. remember

_____ 9. memo

_____ 10. destroy

B

a. recall

b. ruin

c. note

d. allow

e. hurt

f. sightseeing

g. reject

h. build

i. observe

j. learn by heart

k. urge

Antonyms

Match each word in column A with its antonym in column B. An antonym is a word that means the opposite or nearly the opposite and that is the same part of speech. (10 points)

Example: good (adj) Harry's work is very **good**.

You choose: bad (adj) Harry's work is very **bad**.

A

_____ 1. punish

_____ 2. remember

_____ 3. glance

_____ 4. acceptance

_____ 5. decline

_____ 6. praise

_____ 7. encourage

_____ 8. construct

_____ 9. damage

_____ 10. permit

B

a. accept

b. fix

c. destroy

d. reward

e. rejection

f. not allow

g. forget

h. stare

i. advisor

j. scold

k. discourage

Prefixes

In Units 6–10 you worked with several words that used the prefix **re-**. **Re-**, as you remember, means back, again. For example, the word **relive** means to live again. In the following sentences, change the words in parentheses to a verb with the prefix **re-**. Write the new one-word verb in the blank. (5 points)

Example: Bill wants to (live again) his days in the army. <u>relive</u>

1. Please (fold) your test paper (again). _____

2. She (married again) only one month after her divorce.

_____

3. When can you (pay back) what you owe me? _____

4. Our tennis club was (established again) in 1973. _____

5. My teacher says we must (write) each of our papers (again).

_____

Parts of Speech

You may not know these words, but you have studied the suffixes. Write the part of speech of each word **n** (noun), **v** (verb), **adj** (adjective), or **adv** (adverb). (5 points)

_____ 1. visitor

_____ 2. argument

_____ 3. original

_____ 4. reluctance

_____ 5. exhibition

The Right Word

Circle the word which correctly completes each sentence. (20 points)

1. I'm afraid he'll forget our appointment. Will you send him a
   _____?

   remind   memo   memorial   recall

2. I talked to my _____ yesterday, but I'm still not
   sure what I want to major in.

   advice   advise   advisor   advisement

3. Everyday in French class we must _____ ten
   new words before we begin the lesson.

   memorial   remind   memo   memorize

4. I know Kate would enjoy going to Florida with us on spring break, but
   she thinks it will cost too much. I talked with her last night, but she
   _____ to go.

   refused   refusal   rejected   rejection

5. Why don't you try to _____ her to go to Florida
   with us?

   advice   praise   persuade   encouragement

6. If a child does something wrong, I don't spank him. I send him to his
   room. That is the way I _____ him.

   praise   punish   reward   encourage

7. I offered to pay him $5 for driving me to the airport. But he would not
   _____ it. "You can take me sometime," he said
   with a smile.

   accept   acceptance   permission   reject

8. Michael _____ quickly at his watch. It was almost noon: time to leave.

   stared   gazed   glared   glanced

9. Would you like to go _____ with us this weekend?

   resenting   glaring   viewing   sightseeing

10. We plan to _____ Harper's Ferry on Saturday and then Gettysburg on Sunday.

   sightseeing   visit   gaze   glare

Sentences Write one sentence of your own for each word here. Be sure your sentences show the difference between the words in each pair. (40 points)

Example: coward   He is a **coward**.

          cowardly   He is a **cowardly** person.

1. advise _____

   advice _____

2. memory _____

   memorize _____

3. refuse _____

   refusal _____

4. permission _____

   permit _____

5. destroy _____

   destruction _____

6. remind _____

   recall _____

7. watch _____

   gaze _____

8. damage _____

   ruin _____

9. reward _____

   praise _____

10. glare _____

   glance _____

Paragraphs

Write two short paragraphs of your own using these words. You may use the words in any order. Include five or more sentences in each paragraph. (10 points)

1. advisor   remind   encouragement   permit   watch

_____

_____

_____

_____

_____

_____

_____

_____

2. construction   visit   view   permission   persuade

_____

_____

_____

_____

_____

_____

_____

_____

_____

words to learn

unit 11

choose	decision
choice	discover
consider	discovery
considerate	select
decide	selection

unit 12

rely	belief
trust	faith
trustworthy	suspicion
confidence	suspicious
believe	distrust

unit 13

usual	ordinarily
ordinary	frequently
unusual	seldom
abnormal	rarely
special	especially

unit 14

afraid	scary
fear	frighten
fearful	danger
scare	dangerous
scared	endanger

unit 15

pity	sorry
pitiful	patient
sympathy	patience
sympathize	mourn
sorrow	grief

Matching

Match each word with a word that means the same or almost the same. Make sure that the words are the same part of speech (noun, verb, adjective, adverb).

Unit
Key

(12)	_____	1. belief	a. normal
(14)	_____	2. scare	b. find out
(11)	_____	3. choose	c. sad
(15)	_____	4. grief	d. select
(12)	_____	5. suspicion	e. afraid
(13)	_____	6. usual	f. extraordinary
(11)	_____	7. discover	g. doubt
(15)	_____	8. sorry	h. choice
(13)	_____	9. exceptional	i. frighten
(14)	_____	10. fearful	j. faith
			k. great sorrow

Sentences

Write one sentence of your own for each word here.

Unit
Key

(11)   1. consider_____

_____

(11)   2. decide_____

_____

(12)   3. rely_____

_____

(12) 4. believe _____

_____

(13) 5. unusual _____

_____

(13) 6. abnormal _____

_____

(14) 7. scared _____

_____

(14) 8. fear _____

_____

(15) 9. pity _____

_____

(15) 10. sympathize _____

_____

Teacher's Comments:

Units to be Done: 11   12   13   14   15

unit
11

words to learn

choose	discovery
choice	consider
select	considerate
selection	decide
discover	decision

Definitions and Examples

choose
(v)

To **choose** means to pick out or to take something from a group.

Example: I often **choose** a hamburger for lunch.

Example: Tony **chose** John for his team.

choice
(n)

The thing or person you take from a group is your **choice. Choice** also means having the right to choose.

Example: My **choice** is that black puppy with the white paw.

Example: You have two **choices**: study or fail.

select
(v)

To **select** is to pick out or choose.

Example: Devon **selected** a red dress for the dance.

selection
(n)

A **selection** is the thing or person you choose or the action of choosing.

Example: The judges' **selection** of Mary to run for Miss America made her very happy.

discover
(v)

To **discover** is to find out, or to be the first to learn about or find something.

Example: Ann **discovered** that her wallet was missing.

Example: The miners **discovered** gold in California.

discovery
(n)

A **discovery** is the thing you have found, or the action of finding something.

Example: The **discovery** of America was an important event.

Fill in each blank with one of these words.

choose	select	discover
choice	selection	discovery

1. In college each student must _____ (or

_____) a major.

2. Before the _____ of penicillin many people died from pneumonia.

3. The President's _____ (or _____) of a woman as Secretary of the Treasury would make many people happy.

4. Someday they will _____ the cause of cancer.

---

consider*
(v)

To **consider** is to think carefully. It also means to think of someone as something.

Example: Phil **considered** going to Harvard.

Example: I **consider** you my best friend.

considerate
(adj)

A **considerate** person is one who considers others. He tries to help other people and not to hurt their feelings.

Example: The **considerate** man gave his seat on the bus to the pregnant woman.

decide*
(v)

To **decide** means to make up your mind.

Example: Kim **decided** to major in math.

decision
(n)

A **decision** is something that you have decided or made up your mind about.

Example: Sara's **decision** was to buy a Dodge.

*To use these words correctly, you must know these patterns.

1. consider + noun

    consider + verb + -ing

    Examples: I **considered** that **plan** very carefully.
    I **considered going** to the movies.

2. decide + on + noun

    decide + on + verb + -ing

    decide + to + verb

    decide + clause

    Examples: John **decided on** a new **topic** for his paper.
    John **decided on writing** a paper for his course.
    John **decided to write** a paper for his course.
    John **decided that he would fix the bike**.

Fill in each blank with one of these words.

consider   decide

considerate   decision

1. Joe finally made his _____. He will go to Yale, not Harvard.

2. They will _____ taking a trip to New Orleans next winter.

3. They may _____ on Las Vegas for their next vacation.

4. Dave is so _____. He is always helping people.

5. I might _____ to play soccer instead of football this fall.

6. Some people _____ Abe Lincoln our best president ever.

Word-Roots, Word-Beginnings (Prefixes), and Word-Endings (Suffixes)

Lect- is an interesting word-root. **Lect-** means to **choose**. We use it in many English words. Here are some of them:

se**lect**   se**lect**ion   e**lect**   e**lect**ion

The prefix **e-** means **out**. All these words mean to **pick out from a group**.

Also look at the prefix **dis-** which is used in this unit.

discover   **dis** + cover means to **remove the cover** or to **bring out something that was hidden.**

Related Words

discover (v)   consider (v)   elect (v)
discovery (n)   consideration (n)   election (n)
discoverer (n)   considerate (adj)

Using These Words
Circle the correct word in each pair.

choose (v)

considerate (adj)

discover (v)

choice (n)

decide (v)

discovery (n)

selection (n)

consider (v)

decision (n)

select (v)

A student must be very careful when he (choice/chooses) a major. He should (consider/considerate) his interests and skills. He should make his (choice/choose) carefully. If he finds that his (select/selection) was bad, he should try to (discover/discovery) something which will interest him more. At college, a student must (select/selection) a major before he becomes a junior. He can (choose/decide) a major from many different fields. If he is lucky, he will enjoy his studies, and his (considerate/decision) will lead to a job he will enjoy later on.

Read this story.

Lucy got very good grades in high school. She applied to four different colleges. They all accepted her. She thought about going to Oberlin. She had to make up her mind. Finally, she went to Antioch.

We can write these sentences about this story:

Lucy **chose** Antioch.

She **decided** to go to Antioch.

She **selected** Antioch.

Lucy **considered** Oberlin.

Her **decision** was to go to Antioch.

Now read this story.

Terry went to the grocery store. He picked out the things he wanted and took them to the checkout counter. He couldn't find his wallet. Luckily Terry's roommate, Tom, was in the store, too. He paid for Terry's things. On the way home they found Terry's wallet lying on the sidewalk.

We can write these sentences about this story:

Terry took his **selection** to the checkout counter.

He **discovered** that his wallet was missing.

This **discovery** surprised him.

He had no money to pay for his **choice** of food.

Tom was **considerate** when he paid for Terry's things.

They **discovered** the wallet on the sidewalk.

Now write eight sentences about the following story. Use some of your new words. You may also use words from past units.

Carlos needed some toothpaste. He went to the store. He had seen many commercials on TV. The store had many different kinds of toothpaste. First, he looked at the toothpaste that would prevent cavities. Then, he looked at one which would give him whiter teeth. Finally, he looked at one which would give him sex appeal. He did not know what to do. He could not make up his mind. Then a girl came by and quickly picked up some toothpaste. "How did you pick that one?" he asked. "Simple," she said. "It costs fifteen cents less than any of the others."

choose (v)

considerate (adj)

discover (v)

choice (n)

decide (v)

discovery (n)

selection (n)

consider (v)

decision (n)

select (v)

1. _____

_____

2. _____

_____

3. _____

_____

4. _____

_____

5. _____

_____

6. _____

_____

7. _____

_____

8. _____

_____

Write your own paragraph (five to seven sentences) using **five** or more of the new words you have learned. Use any of the paragraphs in this unit as an example.

choose (v)

considerate (adj)

discover (v)

choice (n)

decide (v)

discovery (n)

selection (n)

consider (v)

decision (n)

select (v)

_____

_____

_____

_____

_____

_____

_____

_____

_____

_____

_____

_____

unit 12

rely	belief
trust	faith
trustworthy	suspicion
confidence	suspicious
believe	distrust

Definitions and Examples

rely*
(v)

To **rely** is to depend on (always used with **on** or **upon**).

Example: You can come to me if you need help. You know you can **rely** on me.

trust*
(v)

To **trust** is to be sure of something or someone; to know that you can rely on someone or something.

Example: I **trust** you with my money and my life.

trustworthy
(adj)

Trustworthy means worthy of trust; dependable; reliable.

Example: He has always been a **trustworthy** boy. Even when he was a child, I could send him to the store with $5 and be sure that he would get exactly what I told him to get.

confidence
(n)

Confidence is strong trust.

Example: She has **confidence** in her doctor.

believe*
(v)

To **believe** is to accept as correct or true. To **believe in** is to have trust or confidence in someone or something.

Example: I **believe** what you told me about him.

Example: I **believe** you.

Example: I **believe in** our form of government.

belief (n)	**Belief** is trust or confidence. **A belief** is what you think is true. *Example:* My **belief** in God has never been shaken. *Example:* My parents have **a** strong **belief** in the value of education.
faith (n)	**Faith** is strong belief or trust in someone or something. *Example:* His **faith** in God helped him.
suspicion (n)	**Suspicion** is doubt about someone or something; lack of trust. *Example:* Your **suspicion** was correct. He doesn't wear a ring, but he is married.
suspicious (adj)	**Suspicious** describes a feeling of doubt; a lack of trust. *Example:* She was **suspicious** of him. He said he had to work late, but he didn't answer his phone when she called him at the office.
distrust (v)	To **distrust** is to doubt; to lack trust, faith, or confidence in someone or something. *Example:* Why do you **distrust** me? I have never cheated you.

*To use some of the words in this unit correctly, you must know these patterns.

1. rely + on + (someone or something)

rely + upon + (someone or something)

Examples: I can always **rely on** my friends.
Ben never **relies on** anyone.
You can **rely upon** what I tell you.

2. This pattern means to accept as true or correct.

believe + (someone or something)

Examples: I **believe** his story.
Maceo always **believes** what his mother says.
We **believe** Diane.

This pattern means to have trust, confidence, or faith in.

believe + in + (someone or something)

Examples: James **believes in** democracy.
The ancient Greeks **believed in** Zeus.

3. trust + (someone or something)

distrust + (someone or something)

Examples: Bill **trusts** his friend completely.
Tom **distrusts** his teacher.

Fill in each blank with one of these words.

rely	believe	suspicion
trust	belief	suspicious
trustworthy	faith	distrust
confidence		

1. I _____ Erik to bring the beer.

2. I _____ on my alarm clock to wake me up in time for class.

3. Frank was not sure, but he had a _____ that the salesperson was lying to him.

4. Larry is the most _____ person I know. Let's give him the job.

5. Karen doesn't trust anyone. She is _____ of everyone.

6. You can't believe commercials. I _____ them because they often exaggerate to sell a product.

7. Gordon and Mary _____ that their ancestors were Irish.

8. Different religions have different ideas about life after death. The

   Catholic _____ is that the soul continues to live after the body dies.

Word-Roots, Word-Beginnings (Prefixes), and Word-Endings (Suffixes)

1. You can see the suffix **-ous** in one of the words in this unit: **suspicious**. The suffix **-ous** means **full of** or **having**. A **suspicious** person, then, is someone who "has suspicion" or is "full of suspicion."

2. Another interesting suffix in this unit is **-worthy**. Here you see it with the word **trust**. The suffix **-worthy** gives the idea of **can be**.

For example, if your teacher says, "You are a **trustworthy** student," he or she means that you are "worthy of trust" or that you "can be trusted," or that the teacher "can trust" you.

There are two other words from past units that you could add the suffix **-worthy** to and make a new word:

blame (Unit 1)   blame**worthy**
praise (Unit 9)   praise**worthy**

3. There is a prefix in this unit that you have met before: **dis-**. **Dis-**, as you remember, means **take away**; **not**; **lack of**. If a girl **distrusts** her sister, it means that she does "not trust" her sister, or that she "lacks trust" in her sister.

Related Words

believe (v)		trust (v)
belief (n)	faith (n)	trust (n)
believer (n)		
believable (adj)	faithful (adj)	trustworthy (adj)
believably (adv)	faithfully (adv)	

	rely (v)	suspect (v)
truth (n)	reliance (n)	suspect (n)
truthfulness (n)		suspicion (n)
true* (adj)	reliable (adj)	suspicious (adj)
truthful* (adj)	unreliable (adj)	
truthfully (adv)	reliably (adv)	

confidence (n)		
confident (adj)	untrustworthy (adj)	unfaithful (adj)
		unfaithfully (adv)

*Things are true; people are truthful.

Using These Words
Circle the correct
word in each pair.

rely (v)

confidence (n)

faith (n)

trust (v)

believe (v)

suspicion (n)

distrust (v)

trustworthy (adj)

belief (n)

suspicious (adj)

You can (believe/confidence) what you want, but I didn't do it! Do you

have so little (suspicion/faith) in me? When I took this job, I told you that

the past was behind me. I know I stole money once, but I went to jail for

that. It's over. You have no need to be (suspicious/trustworthy) of me.

Read this. See how
some of the words
in this unit can
be used.

Hidden inside one of the words in this unit, **trust**, is another word. Can you
see what it is? It is the word "true." Many other words in this unit come
from this word-root, "true." Inside the word-root "true" is an interesting
image or picture. "True" comes from the word for tree; true means strong
as a tree. If you **trust** a person, you can **rely** or depend on him or her; this
person is as strong as a tree. A **trustworthy** person is someone you can
depend on and **rely** on because he or she is strong and "true" like a tree.

Now read this story.
See how some of the
words in this unit can
be used.

Sarah wanted to **believe** her husband's story. She knew that marriage
was built on **trust** and **belief** in another person. However, her husband,
Jonathan, had lied to her several times in their first few months of
marriage. He had promised her that he would stop gambling, but she
knew he hadn't. So now, when he told her he had been robbed, she was
suspicious. A quick phone call to the police station proved that her
suspicion was correct. There had been no report of a robbery. Another
lie! How could she have **faith** in him anymore?

Write four sentences about each of the following stories. Use some of the new words from this unit. You may also use words from past units.

rely (v)

confidence (n)

faith (n)

trust (v)

believe (v)

suspicion (n)

distrust (v)

trustworthy (adj)

belief (n)

suspicious (adj)

a. Some people accept whatever other people tell them. They depend on other people to tell them what is right or wrong. Their problem is that they are not sure of themselves. If they were sure of themselves, they would not always accept what other people say.

1. _____

_____

_____

2. _____

_____

_____

3. _____

_____

_____

4. _____

_____

_____

b. Before you can learn to drive a car, you have to know that you can depend on the person who is teaching you how to drive.

1. _____

_____

_____

2. _____

_____

_____

rely (v)

confidence (n)

faith (n)

trust (v)

believe (v)

suspicion (n)

distrust (v)

trustworthy (adj)

belief (n)

suspicious (adj)

3. _____

_____

_____

4. _____

_____

_____

c. The police officer wanted to accept what she said, but he couldn't. All the evidence pointed to her. She was the only person that the old man would allow in the room. He depended on her to give him his daily injection. If the police officer's feeling was right, she had killed him.

1. _____

_____

_____

2. _____

_____

_____

3. _____

_____

_____

4. _____

_____

_____

Write your own paragraph (five to seven sentences) using **five** or more of the new words you have learned in this unit. You may also use words from previous units.

rely (v)

confidence (n)

faith (n)

trust (v)

believe (v)

suspicion (n)

distrust (v)

trustworthy (adj)

belief (n)

suspicious (adj)

unit 13

words to learn

usual	ordinarily
ordinary	frequently
unusual	seldom
abnormal	rarely
special	especially

Definitions and Examples

usual
(adj)

Usual means happening often or seen often. Something that happens often, or is seen often is **usual**.

Example: Our **usual** teacher was sick; so someone else taught our class.

ordinary
(adj)

Ordinary means usual.

Example: On an **ordinary** day, we eat at six o'clock.

unusual
(adj)

Unusual means not usual.

Example: Most people are not as strong as Mohammad Ali. Mohammad Ali's strength is **unusual**.

abnormal
(adj)

Abnormal means not usual, not normal, We use **abnormal** only to describe health, body, weather, or actions.

Example: Fred's blood pressure is **abnormal**.

special
(adj)

Special means very unusual, different in some way.

Example: Christmas is a **special** day for many of us.

Fill in each blank with one of these words.

usual	abnormal	unusual
ordinary	special	

1. The infant had something wrong with his heart. He had a(an)

   _____ heartbeat.

2. The _____ (or _____)
   age for starting school is five.

3. Harry found a(an) _____ stamp in the attic.
   He had never seen one like it before.

4. Jean planned a(an) _____ party for Larry's
   birthday. She wanted to surprise her friend.

5. We paid more than the _____

   (or _____) price for dinner in that fancy
   restaurant.

---

ordinarily
(adv)

Ordinarily means usually.

Example: We **ordinarily** have dinner at six p.m.

frequently
(adv)

Frequently means often.

Example: We **frequently** visit my parents in New York.

seldom
(adv)

Seldom means not often, or only happening a few times.

Example: We **seldom** have veal for dinner. It is too expensive!

rarely
(adv)

Rarely means very seldom.

Example: He **rarely** comes to class. I have seen him only twice this semester.

especially
(adv)

Especially means unusually.

Example: He was **especially** tired after his hard week at work.

Example: He was **unusually** tired after his hard week at work.

Fill in each blank with one of these words.

ordinarily   rarely   seldom
frequently   especially

1. Hector usually gets "A's" and "B's" in his courses. He

   _____ (or _____) gets a "C."

2. I need a lot of sleep; so _____ I go to bed at 10 p.m. That is my usual habit.

3. Antonio is _____ interested in Italy because his father was born there.

4. There are a lot of animals in the woods near my house. I

   _____ see raccoons in the evening.

5. Stella goes to work almost every day. She is

   _____ (or _____) sick enough to stay home.

**Word-Roots,
Word-Beginnings
(Prefixes),
and Word-Endings
(Suffixes)**

Look at these words. See how the prefixes make new words.

unusual   **un** + usual means **not** usual.

abnormal   **ab** + normal means **not** normal.

Related Words

		specialize (v)
normality (n)	abnormality (n)	specialist (n)
		specialty (n)
normal (adj)	abnormal (adj)	special (adj)
normally (adv)	abnormally (adv)	especially (adv)
usual (adj)	unusual (adj)	rare (adj)
usually (adv)	unusually (adv)	rarely (adv)

Using These Words
Circle the correct word in each pair.

usual (adj)

ordinary (adj)

unusual (adj)

special (adj)

ordinarily (adv)

frequently (adv)

abnormal (adj)

seldom (adv)

rarely (adv)

especially (adv)

Tim made many mistakes on his chemistry test. He was very worried and went to see his teacher. The teacher said, "Don't worry about your mistakes; we'll go over everything in class tomorrow. Students (frequently/usual) make these mistakes. Your mistakes are (ordinary/abnormal). They are not (usual/unusual). A few students who have (abnormal/special) ability in chemistry never make these mistakes, but these students are (unusual/seldom). (Rarely/Especially) does a student get 100%. Students (special/ordinarily) make these errors. After we review these problems, I will give a(an) (special/ordinary) test to see if you have improved. This test will be different from the (abnormal/ordinary) test. You should make a good grade on it if you study hard."

Read this paragraph.

Minnesota is very far north. The winters there are very cold. It always snows there in December.

We can write the following sentences about this paragraph:
It **ordinarily** snows in Minnesota in December.
In Minnesota, snow in December is **usual**.
In Minnesota, snow in December is **ordinary**.
It is **especially** cold in Minnesota in December.

Read this paragraph.

Florida is very far south. The winters there are not very cold. It almost never snows there in the winter.

We can write the following sentences about this paragraph:
It **rarely** snows in Florida in December.
In Florida, snow in December is **unusual**.
It **seldom** snows in Florida in December.

Write three sentences about each of the following stories. Use some of the new words from this unit. You may also use words from past units.

usual (adj)

ordinary (adj)

unusual (adj)

special (adj)

ordinarily (adv)

frequently (adv)

abnormal (adj)

seldom (adv)

rarely (adv)

especially (adv)

a. Greg's car is a Volkswagen. It is exactly like most other Volkswagens.

1. _____

_____

_____

2. _____

_____

_____

3. _____

_____

_____

b. Louise bought a new dress. It was very expensive. It was handmade, and no other dress is like it.

1. _____

_____

_____

2. _____

_____

_____

3. _____

_____

_____

usual (adj)

ordinary (adj)

unusual (adj)

special (adj)

ordinarily (adv)

frequently (adv)

abnormal (adj)

seldom (adv)

rarely (adv)

especially (adv)

c. In April there is always a lot of rain in the eastern part of the United States.

1. _____

_____

_____

2. _____

_____

_____

3. _____

_____

_____

d. Mr. Jones was not very athletic. He almost never got any exercise. Last year he learned to play tennis. Now he plays tennis every day.

1. _____

_____

_____

2. _____

_____

_____

3. _____

_____

_____

usual (adj)

ordinary (adj)

unusual (adj)

special (adj)

ordinarily (adv)

frequently (adv)

abnormal (adj)

seldom (adv)

rarely (adv)

especially (adv)

e. Craig felt sick. He went to the doctor. The doctor said that he had a cold. The doctor said that many people have colds now.

1. _____

_____

_____

2. _____

_____

_____

3. _____

_____

_____

Write your own paragraph (five to seven sentences). Use **five** or more of the new words you have learned. Use any of the paragraphs in this unit as an example.

_____

_____

_____

_____

_____

_____

_____

_____

_____

unit 14

words to learn

afraid	scary
fear	frighten
fearful	danger
scare	dangerous
scared	endanger

Definitions and Examples

afraid* (adj)

When you are worried that something will hurt you, you are **afraid** of it. To be **afraid** means to worry that something will hurt you.

Example: Joe is **afraid** of thunder and lightning.

Example: Sue is **afraid** of failing English.

fear (v, n)

To **fear** (v) means to be afraid, to have a worry.

Example: I **fear** snakes.

Fear (n) is a feeling that something might hurt you.

Example: I have a **fear** of snakes.

fearful* (adj)

Fearful means to be full of fear, to have fear.

Example: The **fearful** cat kept away from the big dog.

scare (v)

To **scare** someone means to make him afraid.

Example: The dog **scared** the man.

scared* (adj)

Scared means afraid or worried.

Example: The **scared** rabbit jumped into its hole.

*To use some of the words in this unit correctly, you must know these patterns.

1. be + afraid + of + (someone or something)

   be + fearful + of + (someone or something)

   be + scared + of + (someone or something)

   Examples: I **am afraid of** dogs.
   Bert **is fearful of** new things.
   Tracy **is scared of** ghosts.

2. have a fear of + (someone or something)

   have no fear of + (someone or something)

   Examples: Carl **has a fear** of guns.
   Edna **has no fear** of animals.
   Sally **has great fear of** dentists.
   Bill **has little fear of** snakes.

Fill in each blank with one of these words.

| afraid | scare | fearful |
| fear | scared | |

1. The students had no _____ of failing that course.

2. Do rollercoasters _____ you?

3. Many people are _____ (or _____)

   (or _____) of heights.

4. Mice _____ elephants.

---

scary
(adj)

A **scary** thing makes someone afraid.

Example: The violent thunderstorm was very **scary**.

frighten
(v)

To **frighten** means to scare someone or make him or her worry.

Example: The noise **frightened** the child away.

danger (n)	A **danger** is anything that can hurt, harm, or injure you.
	Example: The grizzly bear was a **danger** to campers.

dangerous (adj)	Something **dangerous** is full of danger or able to cause harm or injury.
	Example: The park ranger killed the **dangerous** bear.

endanger (v)	To **endanger** is to put into danger or to put you in a place where you may be hurt.
	Example: The bear **endangered** the campers.

Fill in each blank with one of these words.

scary   dangerous   danger
frighten   endanger

1. Car racing is a _____ sport. Many people are killed doing it each year.

2. Thunderstorms _____ some people.

3. Airplane mechanics have to be very careful. If a plane loses a part,

   it will _____ many people.

4. Lightning and thunder are _____ .

5. A rockslide is a _____ to the people in that town.

Word-Roots, Word-Beginnings (Prefixes), and Word-Endings (Suffixes)

Look at these words. See how they change.

dangerous	danger + **ous** means **full of danger**. (**-ous** makes an adjective.)
fearful	fear + **ful** means **full of fear**. (**-ful** makes an adjective.)
scary	scare + **y** means **having the ability to scare**. (**-y** makes an adjective.) Notice that we drop the **e**.
endanger	**en** + danger means to **put into danger**.

Related Words

fear (v)	scare (v)	endanger (v)
fear (n)	scare (n)	danger (n)
fearful (adj)	scary (adj)	dangerous (adj)
fearfully (adv)		dangerously (adv)

fright (n)
frightening (adj)

Using These Words
Circle the correct word in each pair.

afraid (adj)

scare (v)

frighten (v)

fear (v, n)

scared (adj)

danger (n)

endanger (v)

fearful (adj)

scary (adj)

dangerous (adj)

1. Ken is (afraid/fear) of snakes. Snakes (scare/fearful) him. His sister says he is too (scary/scared). His (fear/afraid) is silly. Most snakes are harmless. Only a few are (endanger/dangerous). Only poisonous snakes really (endanger/danger) people. Other snakes can't hurt anyone. They can only (frighten/fearful) a person to death.

2. Many people love to see a circus. They admire the lion tamer because he is not (fear/afraid) of lions. The lions don't (scary/scare) him at all. The audience can see the lions' (frighten/scary) teeth and their huge, (dangerous/danger) claws. It is (afraid/scary) to watch the man put his head in a lion's mouth. That is really a (dangerous/danger) trick.

Read this story to see how these words can be used.

Little Miss Muffet is **afraid** of spiders. She has a **fear** of spiders. They **scare** the **fearful** girl. She is **scared** of them. They **frighten** her. Her **fright** makes her run away from them.

Her sister, Little Miss Tuffet, is not **afraid** of spiders. She doesn't think they are **scary.** She is **fearless.** She knows they are not **dangerous.** She knows spiders can't hurt her. They don't **endanger** anyone. They are not a **danger.** So Little Miss Tuffet will sit right beside a spider.

Now read this story.

Peter wants to get good grades. His father gets very angry when Peter gets a low mark in any subject. Peter is failing algebra this semester. He does not want to tell his father.

We can write these sentences to continue this story:

Peter is **afraid** of his father.

Peter **fears** telling his father about his algebra grade.

Peter's father **frightens** him.

Peter will probably lie because of his **fear.**

Peter should not be so **fearful.**

He should not be **scared** of his father.

Write three sentences about each of the following stories. Use some of the new words from this unit. You may also use words from past units.

afraid (adj)

scare (v)

frighten (v)

fear (v, n)

scared (adj)

danger (n)

endanger (v)

fearful (adj)

scary (adj)

dangerous (adj)

a. Al moved to a new room in the dorm. His old room was on the ninth floor. Al did not like that. He could see across the city on clear days. He could also see that he was very far from the ground. He does not like heights. Now he is happy. His new room is on the second floor.

1. _____

_____

2. _____

_____

3. _____

_____

b. It is not safe to drink and drive. Even two drinks can make a person move more slowly. A driver might want to put his foot on the brake quickly but not be able to do that. He might crash and injure himself. He might hit an animal or person crossing the street. It is never safe to ride with someone who has been drinking.

1. _____

_____

2. _____

_____

3. _____

_____

afraid (adj)

scare (v)

frighten (v)

fear (v, n)

scared (adj)

danger (n)

endanger (v)

fearful (adj)

scary (adj)

dangerous (adj)

c. Jim does not like horror movies. He thinks Dracula and Frankenstein are awful. He has nightmares about them. He also hates movies about monsters like King Kong and Godzilla. After he sees one, he thinks he sees a monster on every dark street. He likes only happy films. In the future he will go only to movies made by Walt Disney.

1. _____

_____

_____

2. _____

_____

_____

3. _____

_____

_____

Write your own paragraph (five to seven sentences) using **five** or more of the new words you have learned. Use any of the paragraphs in this unit as an example.

_____

_____

_____

_____

_____

_____

_____

_____

_____

_____

unit 15

words to learn

pity	sorry
pitiful	patience
sympathy	patient
sympathize	mourn
sorrow	grief

Definitions and Examples

pity*
(v, n)

To **pity** (v) someone is to feel sorry for him, or to feel sad for someone who is in trouble.

Example: The girl **pitied** the little lost child.

Pity (n) is a feeling of sorrow for someone who is suffering or in trouble.

Example: We have **pity** for the poor starving people in India.

pitiful
(adj)

Something **pitiful** makes you feel very sad. It makes you feel pity for it.

Example: The wet cat was a **pitiful** sight.

Example: The **pitiful** beggar lived in a house without heat.

sympathy*
(n)

Sympathy is sharing someone else's sorrow. You have **sympathy** for someone when you feel sad because he feels sad.

Example: Sue's grandmother died. Sue has our **sympathy.**

sympathize*
(v)

To **sympathize** is to share someone else's feeling of sadness.

Example: Walter **sympathized** with Tim when Tim failed geometry.

sorrow*
(n)

Sorrow is sadness.

Example: Many people felt **sorrow** when Elvis Presley died.

sorry (adj)	**Sorry** means full of sadness. When you are **sorry,** you feel sad. *Example:* He was **sorry** he had run over the cat.
patience (n)	**Patience** is the ability to accept pain or trouble, or the ability to wait without complaining. *Example:* The teacher had a lot of **patience** with the silly student.
patient (adj)	**Patient** means able to accept pain or trouble or able to wait without complaining. A **patient** person does not complain about pain or trouble or waiting. *Example:* The child was very **patient** as she waited for the grown-ups to stop talking.
mourn* (v)	To **mourn** is to show sorrow, or to feel sad about someone dying. *Example:* The goddess Ceres **mourned** her lost daughter Persephone. *Example:* She **mourned** for one year after her husband died.
grief (n)	**Grief** is sadness, or great sorrow. *Example:* She showed her **grief** by crying for hours.

★To use some of the words in this unit correctly, you must know these patterns.

1. pity + (person or animal)

   Examples: I **pity** that cold little **kitten.**
   Charles **pities** all poor **people.**

   take + pity + on + (person or animal)

   Examples: I **take pity on** that little old man.
   Charles **takes pity on** all poor people.

2. sympathize + with + (someone)

   Examples: I **sympathize with you.**
   Do you **sympathize with** that **man?**

3. have + sympathy + for + (someone)

   Examples: I **have** (great) **sympathy for** you.
   Do you **have** (any) **sympathy for** that man?

   We usually put some word between **have** and **sympathy.** For example, **great, little, a lot of, no, some** may go between **have** and **sympathy.**

4. be + sorry + for + (person or animal)

   feel + sorry + for + (person or animal)

   Examples: I **am sorry for** that poor **man.**
   Kristin **feels sorry for** that little **mouse** in the trap.

5. mourn + for + (someone)

   Example: We **mourned for** our dead cousin.

Fill in each blank
with one of these
words.

pity	sorrow	patient
pitiful	sorry	grief
sympathy	patience	mourn
sympathize		

1. The young child had a lot of _____ for the injured bird.

2. Susan felt _____ for Dan when he struck out in the big game.

3. Americans _____ for John Kennedy and for Martin Luther King.

4. Jenny's _____ at the loss of her hamster changed to joy when she found him under her bed.

5. The _____ woman waited two hours for the bus to come.

6. Hillary showed her _____ at the death of her husband by staying in her room alone for two weeks.

7. Larry cannot wait for anything. He wants everything done immediately. He has no _____ at all.

8. The _____ little child had no home.

9. Do you _____ with the losers on game shows on TV?

10. Kirk and Jan _____ Roland because he is an orphan.

**Word-Roots,
Word-Beginnings
(Prefixes),
and Word-Endings
(Suffixes)**

Look at the suffixes used in this unit.

pitiful　　　　　　pity + **ful** means **causing pity.** Notice that we
　　　　　　　　　　change **y** to **i.** (-**ful** makes an adjective.) This
　　　　　　　　　　is a different meaning of -**ful.** Watch out for it!

sympathize　　　　sympathy + **ize** means to **have sympathy.** (-**ize**
　　　　　　　　　　makes a verb.) Notice that we drop the **y.**

Related Words

sympathize (v)
sympathy (n)　　　　　　patience (n)　　　　　　impatience (n)
sympathetic (adj)　　　　patient (adj)　　　　　impatient (adj)
sympathetically (adv)　　patiently (adv)　　　　impatiently (adv)

mourn (v)　　　　　　　grieve (v)
mourning (n)　　　　　　grief (n)　　　　　　　sorrow (n)
mournful (adj)　　　　　　　　　　　　　　　sorrowful (adj)
mournfully (adv)　　　　　　　　　　　　　　sorrowfully (adv)

Using These Words

Circle the correct word in each pair.

pity (v, n)
sympathize (v)
patience (n)
pitiful (adj)
sorrow (n)
patient (adj)
grief (n)
sympathy (n)
sorry (adj)
mourn (v)

The little dog was a (pity/pitiful) sight. He was sitting on a grave and seemed to be (mourning/sympathizing) for someone. Everyone who saw the dog felt his (sorry/sorrow). They (sorry/sympathized) with him and were (sorry/pitiful) for him. People saw that he would not leave, so they brought him food. They (pitied/sympathized) him because he could not understand that his master was gone forever. They admired his (patience/patient) as he waited day after day for his master to come back. Their (pity/sorrow) could not help him. The (patient/sorrow) dog waited by the grave for 16 years. Finally, he died of old age. He never gave up the hope that his master would return.

Read this story.

Jane is very sad. She is crying. Her best friend, Marge, is leaving college. Marge does not want to leave. She has to go home. Her mother just died. Marge must go home and take care of her ten little brothers and sisters.

We can write these sentences about this story:

Jane is **sorry** that Marge is leaving.

She is crying because of her **grief.**

Jane **sympathizes** with Marge.

It is a **pity** that Marge has to leave school.

But Marge will hide her **sorrow.**

She will be **patient** with her sisters and brothers.

The **pitiful** girl will be cooking and cleaning all the time.

Sometimes Marge will lose her **patience.**

Anyone who takes care of ten children all the time should get a lot of **sympathy.**

Write four sentences about each of the following stories.

pity (v, n)

sympathize (v)

patience (n)

pitiful (adj)

sorrow (n)

patient (adj)

grief (n)

sympathy (n)

sorry (adj)

mourn (v)

a. Almost everyone in the United States felt bad when John Kennedy was killed. People were sad because they had lost a president. They also thought about his two children who wouldn't have a father and his his wife who was left alone. Many people went to Washington to share their loss with others and pay their last respects to this great man.

1. _____

_____

_____

2. _____

_____

_____

3. _____

_____

_____

4. _____

_____

_____

b. Julio wanted to play in the homecoming game. He was not a very good player. He waited for a long time without complaining. He was sad because he couldn't play and because his team was losing. Finally, the coach saw that he really wanted to play. He put Julio in the game.

1. _____

_____

_____

2. _____

_____

_____

pity (v, n)

sympathize (v)

patience (n)

pitiful (adj)

sorrow (n)

patient (adj)

grief (n)

sympathy (n)

sorry (adj)

mourn (v)

3. _____

_____

_____

4. _____

_____

_____

c. We feel sad about students who fail at college. We think sadly about them after they leave here. We hope they enjoy whatever they do after they leave us.

1. _____

_____

_____

2. _____

_____

_____

3. _____

_____

_____

4. _____

_____

_____

Write your own paragraph (five to seven sentences) using **five** or more of the new words you have learned. Use any of the paragraphs in this unit as an example.

pity (v, n)

sympathize (v)

patience (n)

pitiful (adj)

sorrow (n)

patient (adj)

grief (n)

sympathy (n)

sorry (adj)

mourn (v)

Using the New Words

Look at the **new** word in each sentence. Change the **new** word to the correct part of speech to fill in the blank.

Example: Ron Guidry **pitches** for the New York Yankees. He is a

_____.

You answer: <u>pitcher</u>

1. George had to **choose** a new pair of shoes. His _____ was a pair of blue running shoes.

2. Do you **believe** that there are people on Mars? The

_____ in people from outer space is the basis for many movies and books.

3. Many people **endanger** themselves by not wearing seat belts in cars.

Cars can be very _____.

4. Dwayne **decided** to move to New York. He made that

_____ because he wanted to live in a large city.

5. Airplanes are sometimes very late. Passengers have to be **patient,** or

have a lot of _____.

6. We **sympathized** with Tina when she failed her test. We had

_____ for her because she had studied so hard.

7. Columbus **discovered** America. The _____ of America by Columbus opened up a new world to the Europeans.

8. The judges **selected** the winner of the contest. They made their

   _____ of the winner yesterday.

9. Jan and Jill are very **considerate**. They always _____ how other people will feel.

10. You can **trust** Ray. He is very _____ .

Suffixes, Prefixes, and Roots

From your knowledge of the suffixes in these lessons, mark the part of speech of each word here. Write **n** (noun), **v** (verb), **adj** (adjective), or **adv** (adverb) in the blank next to the word.

_____ 1. praiseworthy

_____ 2. hazardous

_____ 3. eventful

_____ 4. legalize

_____ 5. funny

_____ 6. organize

Complete these sentences by underlining the correct choice.

1. The root -**lect**- means _____ .

   allow   choose   decide   find

2. The suffix -**ful** can mean **full of** or _____ .

   having   being   knowing

3. The prefix **e**- means _____ .

   in   out of   into   through

Using the Related Words

Underline the word which correctly completes each sentence.

1. Theresa always tells Maria her problems. Maria is a very _____ person.

   sympathy   sympathize   sympathetic   sympathetically

2. I want to think about your idea. I will give it more _____ .

   consider   considerate   consideration

3. Harold told a funny story about his childhood. The story was probably true. It was a very _____ story.

belief   believe   believable   believably

4. That doctor works only with children. She is a _____.

special   specialize   specialist   specialty

5. The doctor told Paul that he was _____ overweight.

danger   endanger   dangerous   dangerously

6. That child always lies. He never answers a question

_____ .

truth   truthful   truthfully   truthfulness

7. Do you know a _____ mechanic who can fix my car?

rely   reliance   reliable   reliably

8. The children _____ said goodbye to their friends before they moved away.

mourn   mournful   mourning   mournfully

9. The class waited _____ for the teacher to stop talking.

impatient   impatience   impatiently

10. The _____ woman buried her canary in the backyard.

sorrow   sorrowful   sorrowfully

Getting the Right Idea   Read these sentences carefully. Complete the sentences which follow by writing the correct person or thing (noun) in each blank.

1. Walt told Tom a story about Pete. Tom believed Walt's story.
(Choices: Walt, Tom, the story)

_____ is truthful.

_____ is true.

2. Mr. Smith died. His brother, Gerard, felt very bad. Mrs. Jones brought him a cake to make him feel better.

_____ mourned for someone.

_____ had sympathy for someone.

3. Mark had a new watch. Fred believed that Mark had bought the watch. Roberto thought that he had stolen it.

_____ trusted Mark.

_____ was suspicious of Mark.

4. Most people have a temperature of about 98.6 degrees. When someone is very sick, that person's temperature might be about 102 degrees.

_____ degrees is our usual temperature.

_____ degrees is an abnormal temperature.

Writing a Paragraph

Write a paragraph using five or more of these words.

danger	ordinary	believe
unusual	choice	scared
decide	sorry	trust
frighten		

_____

_____

_____

_____

_____

_____

Synonyms

Match each word in column A with its synonym in column B. A synonym is a word that means the same or almost the same and that is the same part of speech. (10 points)

Example: bravery (n)   Cliff's **bravery** surprised all his friends.

You choose: fearlessness (n)   Cliff's **fearlessness** surprised all his friends.

A

_____ 1. select

_____ 2. trust (n)

_____ 3. scare

_____ 4. special

_____ 5. pity (n)

_____ 6. usual

_____ 7. choice

_____ 8. pitiful

_____ 9. dangerous

_____ 10. afraid

B

a. trustworthy

b. frighten

c. sad

d. sympathy

e. ordinary

f. selection

g. harmful

h. confidence

i. unusual

j. scared

k. choose

Antonyms

Match each word in column A with its antonym in column B. An antonym is a word that means the opposite or nearly the opposite and that is the same part of speech. (10 points)

Example: good (adj) Sean's work is very **good**.

You choose: bad (adj) Sean's work is very **bad**.

A   **B**

_____ 1. sorry   a. suspicion

_____ 2. trust (n)   b. wish

_____ 3. ordinary   c. safe

_____ 4. dangerous   d. confidence

_____ 5. grief   e. often

_____ 6. discover   f. unusual

_____ 7. seldom   g. happiness

_____ 8. trustworthy   h. happy

_____ 9. distrust   i. hide

_____ 10. suspicious   j. confident

       k. unreliable

Parts of Speech

You have studied some suffixes and prefixes in these units. Use this knowledge to tell whether each of these new words is a **n** (noun), **v** (verb), **adj** (adjective), or **adv** (adverb). (10 points)

_____ 1. dangerously

_____ 2. sympathetic

_____ 3. dependable

_____ 4. discoverer

_____ 5. realize

_____ 6. obnoxious

_____ 7. mournful

_____ 8. choosy

_____ 9. exception

_____ 10. kindness

The Right Word   Circle the word which best completes each sentence. (20 points)

1. Bill tells Gary his secrets. Gary never tells them to anyone. So, Bill _____ Gary.

   trusts   depends   relies   distrusts

2. Ann always gets "A's" in math. Her _____ grade is an "A."

   frequently   especially   abnormal   usual

3. Students at college do not all take the same courses. Students can _____ the courses they want to take.

   choice   choose   selection   considerate

4. Susan's best friend died last month. Susan still _____ for him.

   fears   sympathizes   pities   mourns

5. Movie monsters are horrible creatures. They _____ people.

   scary   danger   frighten   afraid

6. Evan is at the student bank. There is a long line. Evan must be _____ and wait his turn.

   patience   patient   sorrow   grief

7. Columbus came to America in 1492. Some people say that the Vikings came to America in the year 1000. They say that the Vikings _____ America before Columbus.

   selection   discovered   constructed   established

8. Halloween is the time for witches and goblins. Little children enjoy these _____ costumes.

   fear   scare   scary   afraid

9. Amy has studied hard. She understands her history lesson. She has _____ that she will pass the test.

   believe   trustworthy   suspicion   confidence

10. Dr. Corelli thinks that Fred cheated on the test. He has a _____ .

    suspicion   suspicious   trustworthy   discovery

Sentences

Write one sentence of your own for each word here. Be sure your sentences show the difference between the words in each pair. (40 points)

Example: brave   Arlene was **brave** when she saved the child from the fire.

bravery   Her **bravery** saved the child.

1. suspicious _____

   suspicion _____

2. pity _____

   pitiful _____

3. ordinary _____

   ordinarily _____

4. choose _____

   choice _____

5. fear _____

   afraid _____

6. mourn _____

   grief _____

7. frequently _____

   seldom _____

8. scary _____

   scared _____

9. rely _____

   believe _____

10. consider _____

   decide _____

Paragraphs

For each set of words below write a short paragraph using the words given. You may use the words in any order. In each paragraph include five or more sentences. (10 points)

1. frighten   patient   grief   dangerous   confidence

_____

_____

_____

_____

_____

_____

_____

_____

2. sorrow   suspicious   sympathy   special   scare

_____

_____

_____

_____

_____

_____

_____

_____

_____

words to learn

unit 16

purchase	spend
borrow	expensive
lend	owe
loan	debt
rent	afford

unit 17

reach	acquire
arrive	obtain
arrival	achievement
approach	retain
leave	maintain

unit 18

curious	bother
curiosity	annoy
confuse	annoyance
confusion	irritate
satisfy	nuisance

unit 19

increase	decline
improve	decrease
improvement	reduce
extend	reduction
limit	eliminate

unit 20

conceal	indication
reveal	demonstrate
expose	demonstration
display	define
indicate	describe

units 16-20 pretest

Matching Match each word with a word that means the same or almost the same. Make sure that the words are the same part of speech (noun, verb, adjective, adverb).

Unit
Key

(16) _____	1. purchase	a. annoy
(16) _____	2. loan	b. hide
(17) _____	3. approach	c. make unclear
(17) _____	4. obtain	d. come nearer
(18) _____	5. irritate	e. become less
(18) _____	6. confuse	f. buy
(19) _____	7. increase	g. maintain
(19) _____	8. decline	h. lend
(20) _____	9. conceal	i. show
(20) _____	10. display	j. become larger
		k. acquire

Sentences Write one sentence of your own for each word here.

Unit
Key

(16) 1. debt _____

_____

(16) 2. afford _____

_____

(17) 3. achievement _____

_____

(17)   4. arrive _____

_____

(18)   5. satisfy _____

_____

(18)   6. nuisance _____

_____

(19)   7. improve _____

_____

(19)   8. reduction _____

_____

(20)   9. expose _____

_____

(20) 10. demonstration _____

_____

Teacher's Comments:

Units to be Done: 16   17   18   19   20

unit 16

purchase	spend
borrow	expensive
lend	owe
loan	debt
rent	afford

Definitions and Examples

purchase
(v, n)

To **purchase** (v) means to buy something.

Example: Shari **purchased** a new car.

A **purchase** (n) is a thing which someone has bought.

Example: Jeff carried all of his **purchases** to the car.

borrow
(v)

To **borrow** means to take something which belongs to someone else with the owner's permission, to keep it for awhile, and then return it.

Example: May I **borrow** your math book tonight?

lend*
(v)

To **lend** means to give something to someone to use for a time and then return.

Example: I will **lend** you my suitcase for your trip.

Example: I **lent** my suitcase to Scott last year.

loan
(v, n)

To **loan** (v) means to lend something to someone.

Example: Mineo **loaned** me his suitcase.

A **loan** (n) is anything which is borrowed, especially money.

Example: I need a **loan** to buy a new car.

| rent | To **rent** (v) is to pay someone for the use of something, |
| (v, n) | or to offer someone the use of something for pay. |

Example: We **rented** a car for the weekend from a company which **rents** cars.

Rent (n) is the money a person pays to use something, especially the money one pays to live in a house or apartment owned by someone else.

Example: Our **rent** is due on the fifth of every month.

Fill in each blank with one of these words.

purchase   loan   lend
borrow   rent

1. Mike wanted to _____ his father's car for the night.

2. I paid $25 to _____ a car for the weekend.

3. I need to save enough money to _____ a new bathing suit for my trip.

4. Will you _____ (or _____) me the money to go to Florida?

5. I got a small _____ from my father to help pay for the trip. I will pay him back next summer.

| spend* | To **spend** is to use money or time. |
| (v) | |

Example: I **spend** all of my money each week.

Example: I **spent** $10 for lunch today.

Example: I **spend** every Sunday afternoon at the movies.

| expensive | Something is **expensive** when it costs a lot of money, |
| (adj) | or when it costs more at one place than at another. |

Example: Cadillacs are very **expensive**.

Example: Beer is very **expensive** at that store.

owe
(v)

To **owe** means to have to pay someone for something, or to have an obligation to pay that person. When you borrow five dollars from your friend, you must return it.

Example: You **owe** your friend five dollars.

debt*
(n)

A **debt** is something someone owes to another person, especially money.

Example: People today often have many **debts**.

afford*
(v)

To **afford** is to have enough money to buy something.

Example: He can't **afford** a Cadillac.

Fill in each blank with one of these words.

spend   debt   owe
expensive   afford

1. Diamonds are very _____.

2. I can't _____ to buy a diamond.

3. Don owes Maria money. He has a _____ to pay.

4. Peter and Elizabeth _____ about $100 a week on groceries.

5. Jack bet me that Miami would win the Super Bowl. I won the bet.

   Now he will _____ me $10.

Word-Roots, Word-Beginnings (Prefixes), and Word-Endings (Suffixes)

You know the suffix **-er** or **-or** is used to show the person who does an action. A **runner** is a person who **runs**. Many of the words in this unit can take this suffix.

A **purchaser** is a person who has **purchased** something.

A **renter** is a person who **rents** something.

A **spender** is a person who **spends**. (Do you know the expression: "He is a big spender"?)

A **debtor** is a person who has **debts**. (A long time ago England had special "debtor's prisons.")

There is no rule to help you remember whether a word adds **-er** or **-or**. A few words can use either suffix. An example of that is **advise**. We can write either **adviser** or **advisor**. Both are correct. For other words you must just memorize which form they use.

Related Words

purchase (v)	borrow (v)	lend (v)
purchase (n)		
purchaser (n)	borrower (n)	lender (n)
rent (v)	spend (v)	afford (v)
rent (n)		
renter (n)	spender (n)	
rental (adj)		affordable (adj)
debt (n)	expense (n)	
debtor (n)		
	expensive (adj)	

Using These Words

Circle the correct word in each pair.

purchase (v, n)

borrow (v)

lend (v)

rent (v, n)

spend (v)

expensive (adj)

loan (v, n)

owe (v)

debt (n)

afford (v)

Some people (purchase/spend) more money than they earn. Each month they pay their (afford/rent), next they (purchase/borrow) food at the store, and, finally, they try to make a payment on each of their many (owes/debts). Banks will not (borrow/lend) these people money because the banks are afraid that people who are so deeply in (debt/debts) will never be able to repay the (lend/loan).

Read this story.

Sam just graduated from college. He doesn't have much money. He is living in an apartment and paying $100 to a bank every month for his new car. He seldom goes out on dates because he doesn't have any extra money. He expects to get a raise soon, however; and then he will have enough money to live happily.

We can write these sentences:

Sam **rents** an apartment.

He **purchased** a new car.

He **borrowed** the money for his car.

A bank **loaned** him the money.

It **lent** him over two thousand dollars.

Now he **owes** the bank a lot of money.

His **debt** is very large.

He can't **afford** to go on dates.

He can't **spend** money in restaurants.

Life can be very **expensive**.

Write three sentences about each of the following stories. Use some of the new words from this unit.

purchase (v, n)

borrow (v)

lend (v)

rent (v, n)

spend (v)

expensive (adj)

loan (v, n)

owe (v)

debt (n)

afford (v)

a. Ed has a credit card. He buys a lot on credit. This means he pays a small amount each month. It means he pays interest, or more money in return for using the credit company's money. Now he must pay the credit company $1,000.

1. _____

_____

_____

2. _____

_____

_____

3. _____

_____

_____

b. Sally and Art just got married. They have not decided where to live. They might live in an apartment, or they might buy a house. They have enough money for a down payment on a house, and a bank will give them the rest of the money.

1. _____

_____

_____

2. _____

_____

_____

3. _____

_____

_____

purchase (v, n)

borrow (v)

lend (v)

rent (v, n)

spend (v)

expensive (adj)

loan (v, n)

owe (v)

debt (n)

afford (v)

c. Sharon and Peggy are sisters. They wear the same size. They often wear each other's clothes. Sharon wore Peggy's best blue jeans yesterday. She gave them back today; so Peggy let her wear her new flannel shirt. Peggy doesn't mind. She often wears Sharon's best clothes, too.

1. _____

_____

_____

2. _____

_____

_____

3. _____

_____

_____

Write your own short paragraph (five to seven sentences) using **five** or more of the new words you have learned in this unit.

_____

_____

_____

_____

_____

_____

_____

_____

_____

_____

unit 17

words to learn

reach	acquire
arrive	obtain
arrival	achievement
approach	retain
leave	maintain

Definitions and Examples

reach*
(v)

To **reach** means to come to a place, or to put an arm out towards something.

Example: He **reached** Gallaudet on Tuesday.

Example: The girls **reached** for the ball.

arrive*
(v)

To **arrive** means to reach or come to a place.

Example: She **arrived** here on Wednesday.

arrival
(n)

An **arrival** is the action of reaching a place.

Example: The snow delayed our **arrival.**

approach
(v, n)

To **approach** (v) is to move closer to a person, place, or thing in space or in time.

Example: Jan **approached** the kicking horse carefully. (place)

Example: As graduation day **approached,** we got more and more excited. (time)

An **approach** (n) is the action of coming toward something or a way of coming to something.

Example: The dogs sensed their master's **approach.**

Example: His **approach** to the math problem was all wrong, but he still got the right answer.

leave
(v)

To **leave** is to move away from a person, from a place, or from a thing.

Example: Sheila **left** New York City at 8 o'clock. (a place)

Example: Jill **left** her work on her desk and went to lunch. (a thing)

★To use these words correctly you must know these patterns.

1. When **reach** means **arrive,** it always needs an object. We must tell where or what we **reached.**

   Example: I reached **the mountain top.** (We do not say: reach ⨯ the mountain top.)

   Example: We reached **an agreement.**

   We can also say that we reached **to** or **for** something.

   Example: They reached **for the rope.**

2. **Arrive** may be followed by an adverb (here, there, etc.) or by the word **at** and a noun, or by **in** and a noun, or by **on** and a noun, or by nothing at all.

   Examples: I arrived **there** yesterday. (adverb)
   We arrived **at the beach** at nine. (at + noun)
   We arrived **in London** yesterday. (in + noun)
   The team arrived **on the field** late. (on + noun)
   I have arrived! (nothing)

   Arrive may be followed by the word **home** but by **no other noun.**

   Example: She arrived **home.**

Fill in each blank with one of these words.

reach　　　　　approach　　　　　arrival
arrive　　　　　leave

1. The package I sent will _____ you tomorrow.

2. I don't like this movie. I want to _____ the theater.

3. When the teacher came into the room, the class stopped talking.

   Her _____ ended their conversation.

4. If you want to see the whole movie, then you must

   _____ at the show on time.

5. To touch your toes you must _____ almost to the floor.

6. You should _____ a growling dog with caution.

---

acquire
(v)

To **acquire** means to get something for your own.

Example: When the puppy followed me home, I **acquired** a new pet.

obtain
(v)

To **obtain** means to get something, or to acquire it.

Example: He **obtained** his driving permit last month.

achievement
(n)

An **achievement** is something good which you get through effort.

Example: Dennis worked hard for his college degree. Getting a degree was a big **achievement** for him.

retain
(v)

To **retain** is to keep something which you have.

Example: He **retained** his house in New Jersey when he moved to Florida.

Example: She **retained** her sense of humor even though she was very sick.

maintain
(v)

To **maintain** means to keep something in good condition, or to say something strongly.

Example: Irene **maintains** a small cottage at Deep Creek Lake.

Example: Don **maintains** that Nixon was misunderstood and should become president again.

Fill in each blank with one of these words.

acquire   retain   achievement
obtain   maintain

1. When I was growing up, my family raised collies. I still

   _____ my love for that breed of dog.

2. When I get married, I will _____ a mother-in-law.

3. Some movie stars _____ fame because of their

   unusual hair styles. To _____ that fame they
   must work hard.

4. The man on trial will _____ that he did not steal
   the diamond.

5. I had to go to the bank to _____ some traveller's
   checks for my trip.

6. The old woman swam across the pool. It was hard work for her.

   Swimming across the pool was a real _____
   for her.

**Word-Roots,
Word-Beginnings
(Prefixes),
and Word-Endings
(Suffixes)**

An interesting root in this unit is **-tain** from the Latin word **tenere** meaning **hold.**

I "hold again" or "continue to hold" when I **retain** something.

I "hold by hand" when I **maintain** something. (**Manus** means **hand.**)

I "hold together" when I **contain** something. (**Con** means **with.**)

I "hold from" when I **obtain** something. (**Ob** means **from.**) (I get it from someone else.)

Related Words

reach (v)	approach (v)	obtain (v)
reach (n)	approach (n)	
reachable (adj)	approachable (adj)	obtainable (adj)
achieve (v)	maintain (v)	
achievement (n)	maintenance (n)	

Using These Words
Circle the correct
word in each pair.

reach (v)

arrive (v)

arrival (n)

approach (v)

leave (v)

acquire (v)

maintain (v)

obtain (v)

achievement (n)

retain (v)

Jeff had a busy weekend. He (retain/left) New York on Friday night

and drove to Baltimore. He wanted to (arrive/reach) Baltimore by

11:00 p.m. But as he (arrival/approached) Baltimore, he was stopped by a

police officer. Jeff's license plate was missing. Jeff (maintained/retained)

that he did not know that it was missing, but he got a ticket anyway. The

police officer told him to (achievement/obtain) a new license plate. Jeff's

(arrive/arrival) in Baltimore was not pleasant.

Now read this story.

When Jeff got to Baltimore, he found a burglar in his apartment. He
scared the burglar away. The burglar had put some of Jeff's things in a
bag, but he forgot to take them with him.

We can write these sentences about the story.

Jeff **arrived** in Baltimore.

Jeff **reached** his apartment.

His **arrival** frightened a burglar.

The burglar did not **retain** any of Jeff's things.

Write three sentences
about each of the
following stories. Use
some of the new words
from this unit.

a. Art and Ann will travel from Texas to Florida this week. They will go
from Dallas on Friday and be in Miami on Monday. On Thursday they
will drive straight from Miami to Dallas.

1. _____

_____

_____

| reach (v) |
| arrive (v) |
| arrival (n) |
| approach (v) |
| leave (v) |
| acquire (v) |
| maintain (v) |
| obtain (v) |
| achievement (n) |
| retain (v) |

2. _____

_____

_____

3. _____

_____

b. Jill sent for an application to Columbia University. She got it and filled it out. She wanted to succeed on the entrance test. She got her wish. She will go to Columbia in the fall.

1. _____

_____

_____

2. _____

_____

_____

3. _____

_____

c. Cathy and Karen were college roommates. They graduated five years ago, but they continue to be friends. Their friendship is an important part of their lives. They talk to each other every day on the phone.

1. _____

_____

_____

reach (v)

arrive (v)

arrival (n)

approach (v)

leave (v)

acquire (v)

maintain (v)

obtain (v)

achievement (n)

retain (v)

Write your own short paragraph (five to seven sentences) using **five** or more of the new words which you have learned in this unit.

2. _____

_____

_____

3. _____

_____

_____

_____

_____

_____

_____

_____

_____

_____

_____

_____

_____

_____

words to learn	curious
	curiosity
	confuse
	confusion
	satisfy

bother
annoy
annoyance
irritate
nuisance

Definitions and Examples

curious
(adj)

A **curious** person or animal wants to know about things.

Example: Cats are very **curious** animals.

Example: Kim was **curious** about her grade.

curiosity
(n)

Curiosity is the desire to know about things.

Example: Children want to know about many things. Their **curiosity** is normal.

confuse*
(v)

To **confuse** is to make someone unclear about something.

Example: The teacher **confused** the class. They did not understand what he meant.

Example: Algebra **confuses** me.

confusion
(n)

Confusion is when you do not understand clearly. It is also when things are very mixed up.

Example: The teacher's explanation was clear. It ended the student's **confusion.**

Example: There was a fire in the jail. Many prisoners escaped in the **confusion.**

satisfy*
(v)

To **satisfy** means to fill a person's needs, desires, or expectations.

Example: I was hungry. I ate a big meal. That meal **satisfied** me.

Fill in each blank with one of these words.

curious
curiosity

confusion
satisfy

confuse

1. The new traffic signs have pictures on them. I do not understand

   them. They _____ me.

2. I think I should get a "C" in Health. If I get a "C," my grade will

   _____ me.

3. Builders often put a wooden fence around the place where they are
   working. Sometimes they put small holes in the fence so that we

   can look in and satisfy our _____.

4. When planes are late, many people do not know what to do or how

   to find their friends. There is a great deal of _____.

5. We graduated 10 years ago. We will go to Homecoming this year.

   We are _____ to see what has happened to our
   classmates in the last 10 years.

bother* (v)	To **bother** means to give trouble to someone. *Example:* The ice and snow **bothered** the old man.
annoy* (v)	To **annoy** means to bother. *Example:* The noisy child **annoyed** (or **bothered**) everyone in the restaurant.
annoyance (n)	An **annoyance** is anything that annoys or bothers a person. It is also the state of being annoyed. *Example:* The traffic on Friday night is an **annoyance**. *Example:* He demonstrated his **annoyance**.

irritate*
(v)

To **irritate** means to bother, or to make a person feel angry or annoyed.

Example: The flat tire **irritated** the man.

nuisance
(n)

A **nuisance** is anything which causes annoyance, or which bothers or irritates you.

Example: Younger brothers are sometimes a **nuisance.**

Fill in each blank with one of these words.	bother	irritate	annoyance
	annoy	nuisance	

1. Inflation and high prices _____ all of us.

   (_____ or _____)

2. I left my book at school. I will have to go back and get it. That is a

   real _____ (or _____).

*To use these words correctly you need to know this information.

These words are often used as adjectives. We can make adjectives from many verbs by adding **-ing** and **-ed.** You know that an adjective describes a noun. Here, when we add **-ing** we are describing the thing (or perhaps the person) that makes a person feel some way. When we add **-ed,** we are describing the person himself.

Examples: Measles cause an **irritating** (or **annoying**) itch. The itch makes a person feel **irritated** (or **annoyed**).

The **satisfying** meal started with soup. The meal made the people who ate it feel **satisfied.**

The student got the **confusing** problem wrong. The problem made the student feel **confused.**

The **irritated** (or **annoyed**) man kicked his flat tire. The **satisfied** employee worked hard for his boss. The **confused** student failed the test.

We do not use **bother** in this way. We can *never* write:

The ~~bothering~~ itch. We must write: the **bothersome** itch.

We do not ordinarily write: the ~~bothered~~ man. It is better to use one of the other words instead (that is, **annoyed** or **irritated**).

Word-Roots, Word-Beginnings (Prefixes), and Word-Endings (Suffixes)

Look at these words to see how the suffixes make nouns.

confusion   confuse + **ion** means **the state of being confused.** (**-ion** makes a noun.)

annoyance   annoy + **ance** means **the state of being annoyed.** It is also the thing that annoys us. (**-ance** makes a noun.)

curiosity   curious + **ity** means **the state of being curious.** (**-ity** makes a noun.)

Note: We must change the spelling here. **Curious** drops the **u** = cur**ios** + ity.

We see these same suffixes in other words.

-ion   irritat**ion,** satisfact**ion**

-ance   nuis**ance.** The present form of this root has changed greatly. It is hard to recognize, but it comes from the Latin **nocere** meaning to **harm.** A **nuisance** is something which **harms** someone.

Related Words   bother (v)

	irritation (n)	anoyance (n)
bothersome (adj)	irritated (adj)	annoyed (adj)
	irritating (adj)	annoying (adj)

satisfy (v)   confuse (v)
satisfaction (n)   confusion (n)
satisfied (adj)   confused (adj)
satisfying (adj)   confusing (adj)

Using These Words
Circle the correct word in each pair.

curious (adj)

curiousity (n)

confuse (v)

confusion (n)

satisfy (v)

bother (v)

nuisance (n)

annoy (v)

annoyance (n)

irritate (v)

Registration at school takes a lot of time. Sometimes it is a (curious/nuisance). Standing in long lines is an (annoyance/annoy). It (bothers/satisfies) students to find that a class they want is filled. It (nuisances/irritates) them to have to choose new courses. There is always a lot of (confusion/confuse) at registration time. It is impossible to (satisfy/satisfaction) everyone. The students are always very (confusion/confused) and sometimes a little (annoyance/irritated) when registration is over.

Read this story.

There is an old saying. It tells us that curiosity can get us into trouble. However, if we find out what we want to know, we feel good about it. The saying is: Curiosity killed the cat. Satisfaction brought him back.

We can write these sentences about this story:

The cat was **curious.**

His **curiosity** got him into trouble.

He found out what he wanted to know. That **satisfied** him.

His **satisfaction** made him happy.

Write three sentences about each of the following stories. Use some of the words from this unit.

a. Fred went to the bank on his lunch hour. He found that there was a long line. After waiting in line for half an hour, he found that he had forgotten his checkbook. He could not do his business at the bank.

1. _____

_____

_____

curious (adj)

curiousity (n)

confuse (v)

confusion (n)

satisfy (v)

bother (v)

nuisance (n)

annoy (v)

annoyance (n)

irritate (v)

2. _____

_____

_____

3. _____

_____

_____

b. Many Americans want to know more about life in China. For a long time Americans were not allowed to travel in China. Now that has changed. Americans are able to go to China and find out what life there is really like.

1. _____

_____

_____

2. _____

_____

_____

3. _____

_____

_____

c. Linda did not know what kind of car to buy. One commercial said that Ford made the best car. Another said that Dodge did. Finally she bought a Chevy. Her Chevy runs smoothly. She is happy with it.

1. _____

_____

_____

curious (adj)

curiousity (n)

confuse (v)

confusion (n)

satisfy (v)

bother (v)

nuisance (n)

annoy (v)

annoyance (n)

irritate (v)

Write your own paragraph (five to seven sentences) using **five** or more of the new words you have learned in this unit.

2. _____

_____

_____

3. _____

_____

_____

_____

_____

_____

_____

_____

_____

_____

_____

_____

unit 19

words to learn

increase
improve
improvement
extend
limit

decline
decrease
reduce
reduction
eliminate

Definitions and Examples

increase
(v, n)

To **increase** (v) is to add to something, or to become larger.

Example: The boy practiced shooting baskets every day. His skill in basketball **increased**.

An **increase** (n) is the thing added, especially money.

Example: When she changed jobs, she got a big **increase** in salary.

improve
(v)

To **improve** something is to make it better than it was.

Example: Fred **improved** his van by painting it.

improvement
(n)

An **improvement** is anything which makes something better.

Example: The new paint on the van is a big **improvement**.

extend
(v)

To **extend** something is to make it longer in time or in space.

Example: We went to Florida. We planned to stay for one week. The weather was so warm that we **extended** our trip and stayed for two weeks. (time)

Example: The ladder is six feet long. It can **extend** to ten feet. (space)

To **extend** is also to reach from one place to another.

Example: The bridge **extends** from Maryland to Delaware.

limit (v, n)	To **limit** (v) is to surround an area with an imaginary line which should not be crossed. *Example:* We **limited** each English class to 15 students. *Example:* Brad **limits** himself to two beers when driving. A **limit** (n) is an imaginary line which should not be crossed. *Example:* The speed **limit** is 55 m.p.h.
decline (v)	To **decline** is to become less. *Example:* Washington's population **declined** last year. *Note:* Remember that you learned another meaning for **decline** in Unit 7. There its meaning was **not to accept.**
decrease (v, n)	To **decrease** (v) is to become less, or to decline, or to subtract from something. It is the opposite of **increase**. *Example:* Pollution **decreases** as you move away from the city. *Example:* The landlord **decreased** our rent. A **decrease** (n) is the thing taken away. *Example:* I had a $5 **decrease** in pay this week.
reduce (v)	To **reduce** is to make the number or amount of something less. *Example:* They **reduced** the price of everything for their sale. *Example:* He had too much work to do. He dropped a course to **reduce** his workload. **Reduce** also means to lose weight. *Example:* He was ten pounds overweight and had to **reduce**.
reduction (n)	A **reduction** is the lowering of the amount or number of something. *Example:* Taxes are lower this year. The **reduction** of taxes will help us save money.

eliminate
(v)

To **eliminate** is to throw out or remove completely.

Example: Doctors have **eliminated** smallpox from the world.

Example: Tracy Austin **eliminated** Pam Shriver from the tennis tournament.

Fill in each blank with one of these words.

increase
extend
decrease
improve

limit
reduce
improvement

decline
reduction
eliminate

1. The teacher wanted us to study for the test. She said she would

   _____ it to the last two chapters of the book.

2. The police department is working to _____ crime in this area. There is too much crime here.

3. The ladder will _____ all the way to the roof.

4. Megan's answer was not perfect. It has to be made better. Can

   anyone _____ Megan's answer?

5. The speed limit was 65 m.p.h. a few years ago. The

   _____ of the speed limit to 55 has saved lives.

6. Diamonds _____ in value as time goes on. They become more valuable every year.

7. The old man was unhappy when his wife died. He stopped

   eating. If this continues, his health will _____.

8. A new hairstyle makes a big _____ in his looks.

9. The number of friends that Carol had began to _____ when she was caught shoplifting. They did not want to be with her.

10. Eating out got so expensive that we could not do it any more. We

    had to _____ it from our budget.

**Word-Roots,
Word-Beginnings
(Prefixes),
and Word-Endings
(Suffixes)**

Look at the words in this unit. You see many of the prefixes which you have studied. See how a prefix can change a word.

increase   **in** + crease means **get larger**. (**Crease** comes from a Latin word which means **grow**.)

decrease   **de** + crease means **get smaller**.

Related Words

| extend (v) | eliminate (v) | limit (v) |
| extension (n) | elimination (n) | limitation (n) |

Using These Words
Circle the correct word in each pair.

increase (v, n)

improve (v)

improvement (n)

extend (v)

limit (v, n)

decline (v)

eliminate (v)

decrease (v, n)

reduce (v)

reduction (n)

We used to live near a dirt road which ended in front of our house. Later they (reduced/improved) the road by paving it. They also (extended/reduced) the road to the next highway. This (improve/improvement) made it easier for us to reach the stores in town. But it also (increased/decline) traffic on our road. I am happy that they (eliminated/extended) the road, but I wish that we could (reduction/limit) the number of cars on our road.

Now read this paragraph.

To lose weight, one must diet. This means we eat less food and fewer calories. We must stop eating things like hot fudge sundaes and peanuts.

We can write these sentences about this:

We must eat less to **reduce**.

We must **limit** the calories we eat.

We must **decrease** the amount of food we eat.

We must **eliminate** hot fudge sundaes.

Weight **reduction** can be hard work.

But if we eat sensibly, our health won't **decline** when we diet.

Write three sentences about each of the following stories. Use some of the words from this unit.

a. There is one way to make math classes better. We have 30 students in each class now. We should allow only 20 people in each class. Then the teacher would have time to answer everyone's questions.

1. _____

_____

_____

increase (v, n)

improve (v)

improvement (n)

extend (v)

limit (v, n)

decline (v)

eliminate (v)

decrease (v, n)

reduce (v)

reduction (n)

2. _____

_____

_____

3. _____

_____

_____

b. A curfew requires people to be inside their houses after a certain hour at night. In some places teenagers have curfews. They must be inside after 10 o'clock. People think this will stop crime. There will be less trouble if teens are off the streets at night.

1. _____

_____

_____

2. _____

_____

_____

3. _____

_____

_____

c. Hilda wanted to learn English and worked hard at it. Her teacher could see that she was getting better. Hilda's skill in English grew, but she never forgot her first language. She never lost any of her skill in that language.

1. _____

_____

_____

increase (v, n)

improve (v)

improvement (n)

extend (v)

limit (v, n)

decline (v)

eliminate (v)

decrease (v, n)

reduce (v)

reduction (n)

Write your own paragraph (five to seven sentences) using **five** or more of the new words you have learned in this unit.

2. _____

_____

_____

3. _____

_____

_____

_____

_____

_____

_____

_____

_____

_____

_____

_____

unit 20

words to learn

conceal	indication
reveal	demonstrate
expose	demonstration
display	define
indicate	describe

Definitions and Examples

conceal
(v)

To **conceal** means to hide something or to cover it.

Example: He **concealed** the wine bottle under his coat.

Example: She **concealed** her divorce from her mother.

reveal*
(v)

To **reveal** means to show, or to uncover, or to tell someone something.

Example: Ford **revealed** plans for a new kind of car.

Example: Fran **revealed** the painting she had finished.

expose
(v)

To **expose** means to uncover or reveal something, often with the sense of laying something open to harm, or showing or telling something which another person might have wanted to keep secret.

Example: Joe went outside. He lost his gloves. He **exposed** his hands to the cold.

Example: Watergate **exposed** Nixon's dishonesty.

Example: Sylvia **exposed** Beth's secret.

display*
(v, n)

To **display** (v) is to lay something before someone, to reveal not by telling but by showing.

Example: He **displayed** fear when he ran from the large dog.

Example: All the jewels are **displayed** on the second floor of the museum.

A **display** (n) is a show or exhibit where things are put out for people to see.

Example: The art **display** in the mall is new.

Example: That baseball game was a great **display** of batting skill.

Fill in each blank with one of these words.

conceal   expose
reveal   display

1. It is not good to take new babies into stores. That can

   _____ them to all kinds of germs.

2. We opened the curtain to _____ our snow-covered yard.

3. Drugstores usually _____ many different kinds of lipstick.

4. The child tried to _____ his torn coat from his mother.

5. The teacher made a _____ of all the students' best work.

---

indicate
(v)

To **indicate** means to point out, or to suggest or be a sign of something.

Example: I walked into the classroom. My friend **indicated** an empty desk next to him. (pointed out)

Example: A rash might **indicate** measles. (be a sign of)

Example: The tracks in the snow **indicated** that children had been sledding on the hill. (were a sign of that)

indication (n)	An **indication** is a sign of something. *Example:* All **indications** show that smoking cigarettes is harmful. *Example:* A red sky in the evening is one **indication** that the next day will be pleasant.
demonstrate* (v)	To **demonstrate** is to prove, or show by actual example, or experiment, so that there is no doubt about something or to show how something works. *Example:* He **demonstrated** his anger by slamming the door. *Example:* The salesclerk **demonstrated** the appliance for us. *Example:* Our science teacher **demonstrated** the force of gravity to the class.
demonstration (n)	A **demonstration** is an action which proves something or a presentation which shows how to do something. *Example:* Many people went to see the physics **demonstration**. *Example:* He returned the money he found. That was a **demonstration** of his honesty. *Example:* There was a cooking **demonstration** on TV yesterday.
describe (v)	To **describe** something means to tell about it, to tell what something is like, or what qualities it has. *Example:* He **described** his roommate to his parents. *Example:* The police officer asked Tony to **describe** the car he had seen.
define (v)	To **define** means to explain the nature of something by listing its essential qualities, or to explain the meaning of a word or phrase. *Example:* It is difficult to **define** love. *Example:* Can you **define** "extraneous"?

Fill in each blank with one of these words.

indicate   demonstrate   describe
indication   demonstration   define

1. Fire fighters _____ their courage when they rush into a burning building to rescue a child.

2. Angelo lost his wallet. He called the police. They asked him to

   _____ it so that they could look for it.

3. Some people think that dark fur on caterpillars is a (an)

   _____ of a long cold winter.

4. I won't buy that new camera until I see how it works. I am going

   to the store to see a (an) _____.

5. He had to _____ all the words in his spelling test.

6. Zena did not say that she would go out with Louis, but she did

   _____ that she would.

*To use these words correctly, you need to know this information.

Reveal, **display**, and **demonstrate** can all mean **to show**.

Look at these sentences:

Lamont is afraid of snakes. He saw a snake.

He **revealed** his fear of snakes.

He **displayed** his fear of snakes.

He **demonstrated** his fear of snakes.

These sentences mean that he **showed** his fear of snakes.

Now look at these sentences:

He told me he was afraid of snakes. He **revealed** his fear of snakes.

Only **reveal** means **tell**. Here we *cannot* use **display** or **demonstrate**.

**Word-Roots,
Word-Beginnings
(Prefixes),
and Word-Endings
(Suffixes)**

Look at these words to see how the suffix **-tion** makes each word a noun.

indication   indicate + **ion** means **the act of indicating**.
                        (Notice we drop the final **e**.)

demonstration   demonstrate + **ion** means **the act of demonstrating**.
                        (Notice we drop the final **e**.)

We can also make these words in the same way.

description   describe + **tion** means **the act of describing**.
                        (Notice we drop the **e** and change the **b** to **p**.)

definition   define + **tion** means **the act of defining**.
                        (Notice we change the final **e** to **i**.)

Related Words

demonstrate (v)	indicate (v)	conceal (v)
demonstration (n)	indicator (n)	concealment (n)
	indication (n)	
demonstrable (adj)		
demonstrably (adv)		
reveal (v)	expose (v)	describe (v)
revelation (n)	exposition (n)	description (n)
define (v)		
definition (n)		

Using These Words
Circle the correct
word in each pair.

James used to shoplift. He wanted to (reveal/conceal) the truth from his parents. He was afraid that his recent behavior (indicated/indication) that he was still bothered by the same problem. He didn't know how to (define/describe) to his parents the guilt he felt after he stole something. Each time he walked into a store, he was (exposed/revealed) to another situation where he might (define/reveal) his problem.

conceal (v)

reveal (v)

expose (v)

display (v, n)

indicate (v)

indication (n)

define (v)

demonstrate (v)

demonstration (n)

describe (v)

Read this story.

Our physical education teacher showed us how to do headstands. First, he told us that a headstand is really a stand on the head and forearms. Then, he told us how to start out and how to get our feet in the air. Next, he did one himself to show us how. It looked easy. It wasn't!

We can write these sentences about this story:

Our gym teacher **demonstrated** headstands yesterday.

He **defined** a headstand as a stand on the head and arms.

He **described** the way to get our feet in the air.

His **demonstration** showed us how to do it.

Our teacher's ability **indicated** that it was easy.

That **indication** was wrong.

Now read this story.

Heather and Frank were dating. Frank was 26. Heather was older, but she hid her age from him. One day Frank's older sister came to see them. When she met Heather, she knew her right away. She said, "Don't you remember me? We were in the same class at school." Then Frank knew Heather's age.

We can write these sentences about this story:

Heather **concealed** her age.

Heather did not want to **reveal** her age.

Frank's sister **exposed** Heather's age when she met her.

Write three sentences about each of the following stories. Use some of the new words from this unit.

conceal (v)

reveal (v)

expose (v)

display (v, n)

indicate (v)

indication (n)

define (v)

demonstrate (v)

demonstration (n)

describe (v)

a. There were many demonstrations by students in the U.S. in the 1960's. The students showed their dislike of the war in Viet Nam. They told what life was like in that country. They said the government was hiding the truth. They said that everything suggested that we would lose the war.

1. _____

_____

_____

2. _____

_____

_____

3. _____

_____

_____

b. We have a history test on Friday. We will have to give the meanings of some words. We will have to tell about the Civil War. We will have to show an understanding of the causes of the Civil War. The test will show our knowledge of the Civil War.

1. _____

_____

_____

2. _____

_____

_____

3. _____

_____

_____

conceal (v)

reveal (v)

expose (v)

display (v, n)

indicate (v)

indication (n)

define (v)

demonstrate (v)

demonstration (n)

describe (v)

c. The weather reporter gave a show yesterday. She showed all of the machines and things she uses to help her predict the weather. She explained that some measurements are signs of the way the weather will change. She showed how to use a barometer. A falling barometer might be a sign of rain. A rising barometer usually means sunny skies.

1. _____

_____

_____

2. _____

_____

_____

3. _____

_____

_____

Write your own paragraph (five to seven sentences) using **five** or more of the new words that you have learned in this unit.

_____

_____

_____

_____

_____

_____

_____

_____

_____

units 16-20 review

Using the New Words

Look at the **new** word in each sentence. Change the **new** word to the correct part of speech to fill in the blank.

Example: Ron Guidry **pitches** for the New York Yankees. He is a

_____.

You answer: pitcher

1. A **renter** pays money, or _____, to live in a house.

2. We **arrived** two hours early at the airport. Our _____ surprised the person at the desk.

3. People were **confused** when the subway broke down. There was a lot

of _____ until the subway was fixed.

4. Many children have a lot of **curiosity**. They are very

_____ about the world around them.

5. Fran **achieved** the highest mark in the course. That was a great

_____ for her.

6. Monica studied to **improve** her grade in chemistry. She got an "A".

That was a great _____ for her.

7. Mosquitos are an **annoyance** outdoors. They _____ everyone.

8. The store **reduced** prices for their sale. There was a 50%

_____ in the price of some things.

9. There is a **description** of a coral snake in my book. Can you

_____ the snakes you saw yesterday?

10. Driving a Cadillac is a big **expense**. Gas is so _____ now.

Suffixes, Prefixes, and Roots

In these units you studied some suffixes which make words into nouns. You remember that sometimes you have to change the spelling when you add suffixes. Change each of these words into their root words by removing the suffix and making the necessary spelling changes.

Example: happiness

You answer: happy   (You remove **-ness** and change **i** to **y**.)

1. demonstration _____

2. curiosity _____

3. description _____

4. definition _____

5. indication _____

Match these prefixes and roots with their meanings.

_____ 1. -tain-   a. with

_____ 2. in-   b. hold

_____ 3. de-   c. into

                            d. from

Using the Related Words

Underline the word which correctly completes each sentence.

1. Every school must spend a lot of money for _____.

   maintain   maintenance

2. We lost the game. They will _____ us from the tournament.

   eliminate   elimination

3. The man gave the police a good _____ of the thief.

   describe   description

4. I do not know the _____ of the word "incorrigible."

   define   definition

5. In two months the foreign student made a _____ improvement in his English skills.

   demonstrate   demonstration   demonstrable

6. His _____ of the stolen money made him guilty of the crime.

   conceal   concealment

7. The president could not _____ his plans until he had talked with all of his advisors.

   reveal   revelation

8. The salesclerk's _____ of the car convinced us to buy it.

   demonstrate   demonstration   demonstrable

9. The children missed many days because of snow storms. The Board of Education ordered the _____ of the school year.

   extend   extension   extended

10. Waiting in line is an _____ today.

    irritate   irritation

Getting the Right Idea   Read the sentences carefully. Complete the sentences which follow by writing the correct person or thing (noun) in each blank.

1. Ted gave Dan $2.00.

   _____ borrowed money.

   _____ loaned him money.

2. Joanna is here. Rita is coming.

   _____ is approaching.

   _____ has arrived.

3. Stewart has a 1950 De Soto. He wants to keep it. Art wants to buy it from him.

   _____ wants to retain the De Soto.

   _____ wants to obtain the De Soto.

4. Fred bothers his sister, Jane, all the time.

   _____ is annoyed.

   _____ is a nuisance.

5. Last week bread cost 40¢ a loaf and milk 60¢ a quart. Today bread costs 45¢ a loaf and milk 55¢ a quart.

   The cost of _____ increased.

   The cost of _____ decreased.

Writing a Paragraph   Write a paragraph using five or more of these words.

improve	describe	obtain
satisfy	approach	conceal
spend	reduce	bother

_____

_____

_____

_____

_____

_____

_____

_____

Synonyms

Match each word in column A with its synonym in column B. A synonym is a word that means the same or almost the same and that is the same part of speech. (10 points)

Example: bravery (n)   John's **bravery** surprised all his friends.

You choose: fearlessness (n)   John's **fearlessness** surprised all his friends.

A

_____ 1. lend

_____ 2. acquire

_____ 3. retain

_____ 4. extend

_____ 5. approach

_____ 6. irritation

_____ 7. decline

_____ 8. reveal

_____ 9. confuse

_____ 10. demonstration

B

a. keep

b. annoyance

c. expose

d. decrease

e. make unclear

f. limit

g. loan

h. presentation

i. obtain

j. lengthen

k. come nearer

Antonyms

Match each word in column A with its antonym in column B. An antonym is a word that means the opposite or nearly the opposite and that is the same part of speech. (10 points)

Example: good (adj) Paulino's work is very **good**.

You choose: bad (adj) Paulino's work is very **bad**.

A

_____ 1. decrease

_____ 2. extend

_____ 3. purchase

_____ 4. expensive

_____ 5. arrive

_____ 6. conceal

_____ 7. improve

_____ 8. confused

_____ 9. display

_____ 10. borrow

B

a. shorten

b. cheap

c. display

d. clear

e. increase

f. hide

g. maintain

h. leave

i. lend

j. sell

k. make worse

Parts of Speech

You may not know these words, but you have studied their suffixes in these units. Use what you have learned about suffixes to tell whether these words are **n** (noun), **v** (verb), **adj** (adjective), or **adv** (adverb). (10 points)

_____ 1. arranger

_____ 2. disposable

_____ 3. purity

_____ 4. arrogance

_____ 5. philosophically

_____ 6. realization

_____ 7. arrangement

_____ 8. joyful

_____ 9. concreteness

_____ 10. receptionist

The Right Word   Circle the word which correctly completes each sentence. (20 points)

1. I want to buy a new car. I need to get a _____
    from the bank.

    loan   lend   borrow   owe

2. I didn't have enough money to buy lunch yesterday. I asked Carmen
    for $1. She gave it to me, but I must pay her back the dollar today.
    I _____ Carmen $1.

    loan   lend   owe   borrow

3. I got to school at 8 a.m. this morning. I _____ at
    school at 8 a.m.

    approached   arrival   reached   arrived

4. Neil really wanted a college degree and worked hard for it. He
    _____ his goal when he graduated from college.

    retained   maintained   reached   arrived

5. My teacher is very happy with my work. He gave me an "A". My
    teacher is _____ with my work.

    irritated   satisfied   curious   confused

6. I broke my shoelace. That is a real _____.

    nuisance   confusion   satisfy   annoy

7. Scientists work hard to find the causes of different diseases. For the
    last thirty years they have been trying to _____ polio.

    eliminate   conceal   reduction   improvement

8. A good poker player will not let his face show whether he is happy or
    sad. He does not want to give any _____ of
    whether or not he has a good hand of cards.

    reveal   indication   demonstration   conceal

9. You can go fishing in that lake, but you are allowed to catch only five
    fish each day. The _____ is five.

    eliminate   extend   limit   reduction

10. I need a new driver's license. Where can I _____ one?

    attain   obtain   retain   maintain

Sentences   Write one sentence of your own for each word here. Be sure your sentences show the difference between the words in each pair. (40 points)

Example: careful   Leon is a **careful** person.

carefully   Leon works very **carefully**.

1. afford _____

spend _____

2. arrival _____

approach _____

3. owe _____

debt _____

4. loan _____

borrow _____

5. retain _____

maintain _____

6. curious _____

curiosity _____

7. annoying _____

annoyed _____

8. improve _____

extend _____

9. reduce _____

eliminate _____

10. reveal _____

display _____

Paragraphs

For each set of words below write a short paragraph using the words given. You may use the words in any order. In each paragraph include five or more sentences. (10 points)

1. purchase   loan   expense   owe   afford

_____

_____

_____

_____

_____

_____

_____

_____

2. reach   arrive   arrival   approach   leave

_____

_____

_____

_____

_____

_____

_____

_____

Introduction
Roots, Prefixes, and Suffixes

5
1. prefix
2. suffix
3. root
4. prefix
5. root
6. suffix

6
1. re-   again *or* back
2. ab-   away *or* from
3. un-   not
4. dis-   take away, not, *or* lack
5. en-   in *or* into

6
1. c
2. f
3. e
4. a
5. b
6. d

9
1. -ize   v
2. -ness   n
3. -or   n
4. -al   adj
5. -able   adj

9
1. teacher
2. fearless
3. sunny
4. humorous
5. carefully

Parts of Speech

11
1. girl   ate
   s   v
2. bee   did sting
   s   v
3. couple   ran
   s   v

4. Everyone   wanted
   s   v
5. (phone) book   is
   s   v

13
1. fox   bit   dog
   s   v   o
2. Sara   is playing   piano
   s   v   o
   mother
   op
3. You   did fix   chair
   s   v   o
4. discovery   oil   Alaska
   s   op   op
   helped   United States
   v   o
5. Terry   memorized   words   lesson
   s   v   o   op

15
1. art   adj   adj   n   v
   adj   n   adv
2. art   adj   n   v   art
   adj   n
3. art   adv   adj   n
   adv   v   art   n
4. pro   v   adv   prep
   art   n   prep   art
   adj   n
5. prep   art   n   prep
   art   n   v   art   adj
   n

16
6. art   n   v   art   n
   prep   art   n
7. art   adj   n   v   prep
   art   n
8. v   art   adj   n   v
   prep   n
9. pro   v   art   adj   n
   adv
10. v   art   n   v   art
    n   prep   art   n

Unit 1

24
1. enjoy
2. pleasant *or* delightful *or* enjoyable
3. delight
4. eager
5. delight *or* enjoyment *or* pleasure
6. enthusiastic
7. delightful *or* pleasant *or* enjoyable

26
1. enjoys
2. enthusiasm
3. enjoyable
4. enthusiasm
5. pleasure
6. enthusiastic
7. eager
Answers to other exercises will vary.

Unit 2

32
1. accuse
2. fault
3. accusation
4. blame
5. at fault *or* guilty

34
1. ashamed
2. guilty *or* ashamed
3. guilt *or* shame
4. shameful
5. guilt *or* shame

35
1. accused
2. at fault
3. guilty
4. fault
5. shameful
6. ashamed
7. guilt
8. accusation
Answers to other exercises will vary.

Unit 3

40
1. brave *or* bold *or* fearless *or* courageous
2. brave *or* bold *or* fearless *or* courageous
3. bravery *or* courage *or* boldness
4. bravery *or* courage *or* boldness

40
1. coward
2. cowardice
3. cowardly

42
1. cowardly
2. courage
3. courageous
4. boldness
5. bravery
6. coward
7. courage
Answers to other exercises will vary.

Unit 4

49
1. flammable
2. arsonist
3. ignite
4. glow
5. scorch
6. inflame
7. flare
8. flame
9. blaze
10. arson

51
1. 1) arsonist
   2) blaze
   3) ignited
   4) flammable
   5) blaze
   6) flames

51
2. 1) arson
   2) arson
   3) arsonist
Answers to other exercises will vary.

Unit 5

56
1. honor
2. worship *or* honor
3. regards
4. respect *or* admire
5. respect *or* admire

57
1. resent
2. jealous
3. disregard *or* resent
4. jealousy
5. disrespect

59
1. 1) disregarded
   2) jealous
   3) respect
   4) jealousy

59
2. 1) honor
   2) regard

Unit 5 *(continued)*

59 3. 1) worship
   2) honor
   3) respect
Answers to other exercises will vary.

Unit 6

80 1. memorize *or* remember *or* recall
   2. recall *or* remember
   3. relive
   4. memory
   5. recall *or* remember

82 1. reminder *or* memorandum *or* memo
   2. memorial
   3. remind
   4. reminder
   5. memorandum

83 1. 1) remember
   2) Memorial
   3) reminded
   4) memorized
   5) recalled
83 2. 1) memo
   2) memorandum
83 3. 1) memories
   2) remember
   3) recall
   4) relive
Answers to other exercises will vary.

Unit 7

89 1. permission
   2. accept
   3. permit *or* allow
   4. decline *or* refuse
   5. acceptance
   6. refuse
   7. refusal

91 1. permit
   2. allow
   3. allowed
   4. refused
   5. declined
   6. rejected
   7. acceptance
   8. rejection
Answers to other exercises will vary.

Unit 8

96 1. observe
   2. watch *or* view
   3. inspect
   4. sightseeing
   5. view
   6. visit

98 1. gaze
   2. stare *or* gaze
   3. glance
   4. glare

100 1. 1) watch
   2) stare
   3) sightseeing
   4) visit
100 2. 1) glanced
   2) observed
   3) glance
   4) observed
   5) glared
   6) watch
Answers to other exercises will vary.

Unit 9

106 1. advisor
   2. persuade
   3. encourage
   4. advise *or* encourage
   5. advice
   6. encouragement

107 1. reward
   2. punish
   3. scold
   4. praise

109 1. 1) encouragement
   2) encouraged
   3) advice
   2. 1) scold
   2) punish
   3) praise
   4) reward
Answers to other exercises will vary.

Unit 10

114 1. destroy
   2. damage
   3. disaster
   4. injure
   5. ruin

Unit 10 *(continued)*

115
1. construct
2. establishment
3. establish
4. construction

116
1. disaster
2. destroyed
3. destruction
4. ruined
5. established
6. construct
7. construction
8. establishment
9. injured
10. destruction
Answers to other exercises will vary.

Unit 11

136
1. choose *or* select
2. discovery
3. choice *or* selection
4. discover

137
1. decision
2. consider
3. decide
4. considerate
5. decide
6. consider

139
1. chooses
2. consider
3. choice
4. selection
5. discover
6. select
7. choose
8. decision
Answers to other exercises will vary.

Unit 12

146
1. trust
2. rely
3. suspicion
4. trustworthy
5. suspicious
6. distrust
7. believe
8. belief

148
1. believe
2. faith
3. suspicious
Answers to other exercises will vary.

Unit 13

154
1. abnormal
2. usual *or* ordinary
3. unusual *or* special
4. special
5. usual *or* ordinary

155
1. seldom *or* rarely
2. ordinarily *or* frequently
3. especially
4. frequently *or* ordinarily
5. seldom *or* rarely

157
1. frequently
2. ordinary
3. unusual
4. special
5. unusual
6. rarely
7. ordinarily
8. special
9. ordinary
Answers to other exercises will vary.

Unit 14

162
1. fear
2. scare
3. afraid *or* fearful *or* scared
4. scare

163
1. dangerous *or* scary
2. frighten *or* endanger
3. endanger *or* frighten
4. scary *or* dangerous
5. danger

165
1. 1) afraid
   2) scare
   3) scared
   4) fear
   5) dangerous
   6) endanger
   7) frighten

Unit 14 *(continued)*

165 2. 1) afraid
2) scare
3) scary
4) dangerous
5) scary
6) dangerous
Answers to other exercises will vary.

Unit 15

172 1. sympathy *or* sorrow *or* pity
2. sorry
3. mourn
4. sorrow
5. patient
6. grief
7. patience
8. pitiful
9. sympathize
10. pity

174 1. pitiful
2. mourning
3. sorrow
4. sympathized
5. sorry
6. pitied
7. patience
8. pity
9. patient
Answers to other exercises will vary.

Unit 16

194 1. borrow
2. rent
3. purchase
4. lend *or* loan
5. loan

195 1. expensive
2. afford
3. debt
4. spend
5. owe

197 1. spend
2. rent
3. purchase
4. debts
5. lend
6. debt
7. loan
Answers to other exercises will vary.

Unit 17

203 1. reach
2. leave
3. arrival
4. arrive
5. reach
6. approach

204 1. retain
2. obtain *or* acquire
3. acquire *or* maintain
4. maintain
5. acquire *or* obtain
6. achievement

206 1. left
2. reach
3. approached
4. maintained
5. obtain
6. arrival
Answers to other exercises will vary.

Unit 18

210 1. confuse
2. satisfy
3. curiosity
4. confusion
5. curious

211 1. annoy *or* bother *or* irritate
2. annoyance *or* nuisance

214 1. nuisance
2. annoyance
3. bothers
4. irritates
5. confusion
6. satisfy
7. confused
8. irritated
Answers to other exercises will vary.

Unit 19

220 1. limit
2. reduce
3. extend
4. improve
5. reduction
6. increase
7. decline

Unit 19 *(continued)*

220   8. improvement
   9. decrease
   10. eliminate

222   1. improved
   2. extended
   3. improvement
   4. increased
   5. extended
   6. limit
Answers to other exercises will vary.

Unit 20

226   1. expose
   2. reveal
   3. display
   4. conceal
   5. display

228   1. demonstrate
   2. describe
   3. indication
   4. demonstration
   5. define
   6. indicate

230   1. conceal
   2. indicated
   3. describe
   4. exposed
   5. reveal
Answers to other exercises will vary.

PRETEST UNITS 1-5

Matching

19
1. k
2. b
3. g
4. e
5. i
6. d
7. a
8. c
9. h
10. f

Sentences 1-10 will vary.

REVIEW UNITS 1-5

Using the New Words

63
1. brave
2. jealous
3. arsonist
4. cowardly
5. delightful
6. accusation
7. ashamed
8. guilty

64
9. pleasant
10. enthusiasm

Suffixes, Prefixes, and Roots

Matching

64
1. d
2. a
3. b
4. c

Parts of Speech

64
1. adj
2. adj
3. n
4. n
5. adj
6. n
7. adj
8. adj
9. adj
10. n

Using the Related Words

64
1. delightfully
2. please

65
3. shamefully
4. admire
5. disrespectful
6. boldly
7. unpleasantly
8. eagerly
9. fearlessly
10. honorable

Getting the Right Idea

65
1. Dale—Philip

66
2. Randy—Stealing
3. crime—Lou
4. Tim—Frank
5. Mark—Terry

Paragraphs will vary.

POST TEST UNITS 1-5

Synonyms

67
1. c
2. e
3. g
4. j
5. a
6. b
7. d
8. k
9. h
10. i

Antonyms

68
1. b
2. k
3. e
4. i
5. f
6. h
7. d
8. c
9. j
10. a

Parts of Speech

68
1. adj
2. adv
3. adj
4. adj
5. n
6. adj
7. n
8. adj
9. adj
10. n

The Right Word

69
1. enjoyable
2. ignite
3. shameful
4. brave
5. admire
6. at fault
7. eager
8. flammable
9. respect
10. scorched
Sentences 1-10 will vary.
Paragraphs will vary.

PRETEST UNITS 6-10

Matching

75
1. g
2. i
3. a
4. j
5. e
6. c
7. b
8. d
9. h
10. k

Fill in the Blank

76
1. praise
2. scold
3. reward
4. punish
Sentences 1-10 will vary.

REVIEW UNITS 6-10

Using the New Words

119
1. memorize
2. permission
3. reminder
4. acceptance
5. advice

6. destroy
7. reject
8. refusal
120 9. encouragement
10. construct

Suffixes, Prefixes, and Roots
Matching
120
1. c
2. e
3. b
4. a
5. d

Parts of Speech
120
1. n
2. n
3. v
4. n
5. adj
6. n
7. v
8. n

Using the Related Words
120
1. persuasively
2. inspection
121
3. observation
4. acceptable
5. commemorate
6. dejected
7. persuade
8. re-establish
9. discourage
10. view

Getting the Right Idea
121
1. Joe—Ed
122
2. Ann—Fran
3. Barry—Clyde
4. orange—lemon
5. Dan—Earl
Paragraphs will vary.

POST TEST UNITS 6-10

Synonyms
125
1. d
2. i
3. h
4. k
5. j
6. g
7. e
8. a
9. c
10. b

Antonyms

126
1. d
2. g
3. h
4. e
5. a
6. j
7. k
8. c
9. b
10. f

Prefixes

126
1. refold
2. remarried
3. repay
4. re-established
5. rewrite

Parts of Speech

127
1. n
2. n
3. adj
4. n
5. n

The Right Word

127
1. memo
2. advisor
3. memorize
4. refused
5. persuade
6. punish
7. accept

128
8. glanced
9. sightseeing
10. visit
Sentences 1-10 will vary.
Paragraphs will vary.

PRETEST UNITS 11-15

Matching

133
1. j
2. i
3. d
4. k
5. g
6. a
7. b
8. c
9. f
10. e
Sentences 1-10 will vary.

REVIEW UNITS 11-15

Using the New Words

179
1. choice
2. belief
3. dangerous
4. decision
5. patience
6. sympathy
7. discovery

180
8. selection
9. consider
10. trustworthy

Suffixes, Prefixes, and Roots
Parts of Speech

180
1. adj
2. adj
3. adj
4. v
5. adj
6. v

The Right Word

180
1. choose
2. having
3. out of

Using the Related Words

180
1. sympathetic
2. consideration

181
3. believable
4. specialist
5. dangerously
6. truthfully
7. reliable
8. mournfully
9. impatiently
10. sorrowful

Getting the Right Idea

181
1. Walt—story

182
2. Gerard—Mrs. Jones
3. Fred—Roberto
4. 98.6—102
Paragraphs will vary.

POST TEST UNITS 11-15

Synonyms

183
1. k
2. h
3. b
4. i
5. d
6. e

Synonyms (continued)
183   7. f
      8. c
      9. g
      10. j

Antonyms
184   1. h
      2. a
      3. f
      4. c
      5. g
      6. i
      7. e
      8. k
      9. d
      10. j

Parts of Speech
184   1. adv
      2. adj
      3. adj
      4. n
      5. v
      6. adj
      7. adj
      8. adj
      9. n
      10. n

The Right Word
185   1. trusts
      2. usual
      3. choose
      4. mourns
      5. frighten
      6. patient
      7. discovered
      8. scary
      9. confidence
      10. suspicion
Sentences 1-10 will vary.
Paragraphs will vary.

PRETEST UNITS 16-20

Matching
191   1. f
      2. h
      3. d
      4. k
      5. a
      6. c
      7. j
      8. e

9. b
10. i
Sentences 1-10 will vary.

REVIEW UNITS 16-20

Using the New Words
233   1. rent
      2. arrival
      3. confusion
      4. curious
      5. achievement
      6. improvement
      7. annoy
234   8. reduction
      9. describe
      10. expensive

Suffixes, Prefixes, and Roots
234   1. demonstrate
      2. curious
      3. describe
      4. define
      5. indicate
Matching
234   1. b
      2. c
      3. d

Using the Related Words
235   1. maintenance
      2. eliminate
      3. description
      4. definition
      5. demonstrable
      6. concealment
      7. reveal
      8. demonstration
      9. extension
      10. irritation

Getting the Right Idea
236   1. Dan—Ted
      2. Rita—Joanna
      3. Stewart—Art
      4. Jane—Fred
      5. bread—milk
Paragraphs will vary.

POST TEST UNITS 16-20

Synonyms
239   1. g
      2. i
      3. a

Synonyms (continued)

239
4. j
5. k
6. b
7. d
8. c
9. e
10. h

Antonyms

240
1. e
2. a
3. j
4. b
5. h
6. c
7. k
8. d
9. f
10. i

Parts of Speech

240
1. n
2. adj
3. n
4. n
5. adv
6. n
7. n
8. adj
9. n
10. n

The Right Word

241
1. loan
2. owe
3. arrived
4. reached
5. satisfied
6. nuisance
7. eliminate
8. indication
9. limit
10. obtain
Sentences 1-10 will vary.
Paragraphs will vary.

index

This index includes all the new words and related words with the unit number in which they are first taught. New words are printed in **boldface.**

decision (n)	11	**extend** (v)	19
decline (v)	7, 19	extension (n)	19
decrease (v)	19		
define (v)	20	**faith** (n)	12
definition (n)	20	faithful (adj)	12
delight (v,n)	1	faithfully (adv)	12
delightful (adj)	1	**fault** (n)	2
delightfully (adv)	1	**at fault** (adj)	2
demonstrable (adj)	20	**fear** (v,n)	14
demonstrably (adv)	20	**fearful** (adj)	14
demonstrate (v)	20	fearfully (adv)	14
demonstration (n)	20	**fearless** (adj)	3
describe (v)	20	fearlessly (adv)	3
description (n)	20	fearlessness (n)	3
destroy (v)	10	**flame** (n)	4
destruction (n)	10	**flammable** (adj)	4
destructive (adj)	10	**flare** (v,n)	4
disaster (n)	10	frequent (adj)	13
discourage (v)	3, 9	**frequently** (adv)	13
discouragement (n)	3, 9	fright (n)	14
discouraging (adj)	3, 9	**frighten** (v)	14
discover (v)	11	frightening (adj)	14
discoverer (n)	11		
discovery (n)	11	**gaze** (v)	8
dishonor (v,n)	5	**glance** (v,n)	8
dishonorable (adj)	5	**glare** (n)	8
dishonorably (adv)	5	**glow** (v)	4
display (v,n)	20	**grief** (n)	15
disregard (v,n)	5	grieve (v)	15
disrespect (v)	5	**guilt** (n)	2
disrespectful (adj)	5	**guilty** (adj)	2
disrespectfully (adv)	5		
distrust (v,n)	12	**honor** (v,n)	5
		honorable (adj)	5
		honorably (adv)	5
eager (adj)	1		
eagerly (adv)	1	**ignite** (v)	4
eagerness (n)	1	impatience (n)	15
elect (v)	11	impatient (adj)	15
election (n)	11	impatiently (adv)	15
eliminate (v)	19	**improve** (v)	19
elimination (n)	19	**improvement** (n)	19
eject (v)	7	**increase** (v)	19
ejection (n)	7	**indicate** (v)	20
encourage (v)	9	**indication** (n)	20
encouragement (n)	9	indicator (n)	20
encouraging (adj)	9	**inflame** (v)	4
encouragingly (adv)	9	inject (v)	7
endanger (v)	14	injection (n)	7
enjoy (v)	1	**injure** (v)	10
enjoyable (adj)	1	injury (n)	10
enjoyment (n)	1	**inspect** (v)	8
enthusiasm (n)	1	inspection (n)	8
enthusiastic (adj)	1	inspector (n)	8
enthusiastically (adv)	1	**irritate** (v)	18
establish (v)	10	irritated (adj)	18
establishment (n)	10	irritating (adj)	18
expense (n)	16	irritation (n)	18
expensive (adj)	16		
especially (adv)	13	**jealous** (adj)	5
expose (v)	20	jealously (adv)	5
exposition (n)	20	**jealousy** (n)	5

ONCE IN FAIR VERONA there lived two families who had fought for so long that no one could remember why their quarrel first began. Now whenever the Montagues and the Capulets met in the streets, a battle was sure to follow. Thus it was one summer's day when a sharp word and a rude gesture quickly led to drawn swords and a building brawl.

Into the fight rode Prince Escalus. "Rebellious subjects! Enemies to peace! Throw your weapons to the ground and hear my sentence: If ever you disturb our streets again, your lives shall be the price."

As the crowd cleared, Lord Montague spotted his nephew, gentle Benvolio. "Who began the fight this time?" the lord asked.

"It was raging among the servants when I arrived," replied Benvolio. "I drew my sword to part them, but fiery Tybalt came storming in for the Capulets, making the battle all the worse."

"What of Romeo?" asked Lady Montague anxiously. "Have you seen my son?"

"Aye, just before dawn. But he looked most mournful and ducked away, so I did not pursue him."

"He has been this way much of late," said Lord Montague. "He weeps in the morning, and locks himself away in his room, making for himself an artificial night. But I cannot learn the cause."

"I will do what I can to discover it," promised Benvolio. And indeed, when he found his cousin, it was not hard to learn the source of Romeo's despair. He was in love.

Alas, the one he loved did not love him back.

"Love is a smoke made with the fume of sighs," he moaned. "A madness most discreet, a choking gall. I am shut up in prison, whipped and tormented. I am—"

"Peace," said Benvolio, taking his cousin by the arm. "There is to be a feast tonight at the home of the Capulets. Let us go masked and make a merry time of it."

Romeo did not feign even slight interest, but Benvolio continued. "Rosaline, whom you love but are loved not by, will be there. Compare her face with some that I shall show, and I will make thee think thy swan a crow!"

"I will go," sighed Romeo. "But only for the chance to gaze on fair Rosaline."

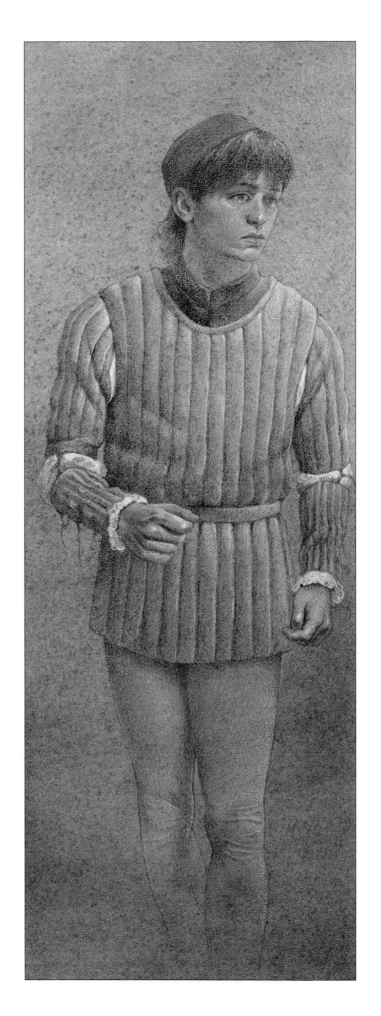

As the hour for the party drew near, Lady Capulet went to speak with her daughter, a fair maid named Juliet who had yet to see her fourteenth birthday. "Tell me, Daughter," said the lady, "how stands your disposition to be married?"

"It is an honour I dream not of," said Juliet.

"Well, think on it now, for I come with great news. The gallant Count Paris seeks you for his love."

"O such a man!" cried Juliet's nurse. "A very flower of manhood!"

"Hush, Nurse," said Lady Capulet. "What say you, Juliet? Can you love the gentleman? This night you shall see him at our feast. Read over the volume of his face and see what's written there."

"I'll study it with care," said Juliet softly.

The barest hint of moonlight dusted Verona's streets as Romeo, Benvolio, and their friend Mercutio headed for the party.

"Give me a torch," said Romeo. "Being heavy, I will bear the light."

"Nay, we must have you dance!" cried Mercutio.

"Not I," protested Romeo. "*You* have dancing shoes with nimble soles; *I* have a soul of lead."

"You are a lover!" teased Mercutio, capering about him. "Borrow Cupid's wings and soar!"

"Peace, Mercutio," said Romeo. "You talk of nothing."

"And you talk too much," chided Benvolio. "Supper is done, and we shall arrive too late."

"Perhaps too early," said Romeo. He looked into the night sky and shuddered. "My mind misgives some consequence yet hanging in the stars shall bitterly begin this fearful night. But onward! I'll not a coward be."

And so they donned their masks and entered in. And there, as Romeo searched among the dancing ladies for a sight of Rosaline, his eye fell instead on Juliet. In that instant all thought of past love vanished. "O she doth teach the torches to burn bright," he murmured. "Beauty too rich for use, for Earth too dear."

The fierce Tybalt stood nearby and recognized Romeo's voice. "How dare a Montague intrude on this gathering," he growled. "By the stock and honour of my kin, to strike him dead I hold it not a sin."

But his uncle warned him to hold his anger. "Here in my house we will have no quarrel this night," said Lord Capulet. "Now go to, boy!"

"I *leave*, but I do not *forget*," said Tybalt.

Romeo, still in his trance, approached Juliet. As he held out his hand to dance, he whispered, "If I profane with my unworthiest hand this holy shrine, the gentle sin is this: My lips, two blushing pilgrims, ready stand to smooth that rough touch with a tender kiss."

Juliet glanced down, then slowly raised her eyes to his. With a shy smile she replied, "Good pilgrim, you do wrong your hand too much."

Then they entered the dance — eyes locked on each other and fingers entwined, as if there were no one else in the room. Before the music stopped, they swept themselves to a private place, and shared a tender kiss.

Alas, the moment was broken by Juliet's nurse. "Madam, your mother craves a word with you."

"Who is her mother?" asked Romeo when Juliet had gone.

"The lady of the house," the nurse proudly replied.

"A Capulet?" Romeo shuddered as the nurse bustled off. "I have given my heart to mine enemy!"

As the guests began to depart, Juliet called the nurse aside. She asked after the names of several young men, hiding her true desire to learn only one. When she did, she was as horrified as Romeo had been. "My only love," she moaned, "sprung from my only hate!"

Romeo slipped away from his friends as they left the party. He climbed the wall of old Capulet's orchard and stood outside the house. A window opened. Juliet stepped on to her balcony.

"What light through yonder window breaks?" whispered Romeo. "It is the East, and Juliet is the Sun."

"O Romeo, Romeo," said Juliet to the night. "'Tis but thy name that is my enemy. What's in a name? That which we call a rose by any other word would smell as sweet. Discard thy name, which is no part of thee, and in return take all myself."

Romeo could keep still no longer. "I take thee at thy word. Call me but love, and henceforth I never will be Romeo."

Juliet put her hand to her heart. "My ears have not yet drunk a hundred words of thy tongue's uttering, yet I know the sound. Art thou not Romeo, and a Montague?"

"Neither, fair maid, if either thee dislike."

"If my kinsmen see thee, they will murder thee."

"Alack, there lies more peril in thine eye than twenty of their swords!"

Juliet smiled and leaned down. The night was warm and sweet, the scent of ripening fruit filled the air, insects sang their darktime songs. And here in this time out of time, the young lovers exchanged many tender words.

All too soon the nurse called out for Juliet.

"I must go," she whispered. "But if your intentions be honest, your purpose marriage, then give word to one I will send to you tomorrow. Say when and where we shall wed, and I will follow thee throughout the world."

"Juliet!" cried the nurse.

"I must go *now*. O good night, good night. Parting is such sweet sorrow that I shall say good night till it be morrow."

At dawn Romeo went to seek Friar Lawrence – his friend, advisor and confessor. As usual, the old monk was out gathering herbs for his medicines.

"Romeo!" cried the friar in delight. "Why are you up so early?" He looked at the youth suspiciously. "Or have you not yet been to bed this night?"

"It's true! I have been feasting with my enemy, where I met one whom I love more than all the Earth."

"What of Rosaline?"

"She is nothing to me! Juliet is all my love. Better yet, she loves me back. Will you marry us?"

"Wisely and slow, my lad," said the friar. "They stumble that run fast." He studied Romeo for a moment, then added, "And yet, I will help you in this cause for one reason: By this marriage we may put an end to the war between your houses."

As the sun climbed higher in the sky, Mercutio and Benvolio roamed the city, looking for their friend. "He came not home last night," said Benvolio, "for I've been to seek him. What did come was a letter to Romeo, sent by Tybalt."

"A challenge!" crowed Mercutio. "And look, here's the one to be challenged. Romeo, you gave us the slip last night!"

"I gave you no slip," said Romeo. "You'll have to find your own!"

Mercutio slapped his thigh. "Why, here's the old Romeo! And a better one by far than yesterday's droopy, lovesick child."

Just then Juliet's nurse came scurrying up the street. Romeo was at her side at once. "What word do you bring?"

The nurse studied him. "Are your intentions honourable?"

Romeo smiled. "Bid your mistress come to Friar Lawrence this afternoon, and there she will be wed. Does that answer your question?"

"Aye, it does, and answers it well."

And so it was set. Romeo and Juliet met with Friar Lawrence, who performed the holy ceremony in secret. Never was a happier bride, never a more loving groom. And never were two sadder to part.

"Tonight," whispered Romeo. "I'll come to thee tonight."

But as Romeo started home through the afternoon heat, he found his friends fending off a quarrel with Tybalt. When the young hotblood spotted Romeo, he cried, "There you are, you villain!"

Romeo had no wish to quarrel with his new wife's cousin. "I am no villain," he said mildly. "Indeed, I now have more cause to love you than you can imagine." Tybalt continued to mock and taunt, but Romeo walked away.

"O mild submission," groaned Mercutio. "Tybalt, you rat-catcher, will you try your hand with me?"

In an instant, swords were out, their steel flashing in the sun. The street rang with the sound of battle.

"Wait!" Romeo yelled, turning back. "The prince has forbidden this!" He plunged between them. As he did, Tybalt's sword passed beneath Romeo's arm. Mercutio cried out and staggered. Tybalt withdrew his reddened blade, and stood staring at it in horror.

Romeo and Benvolio helped their friend to a resting place. "Courage, man," said Romeo. "The hurt cannot be much."

"No," gasped Mercutio. "'Tis not so deep as a well, nor so wide as a church door, but 'tis enough, 'twill serve." Death crept closer, and Mercutio clutched Romeo's shirt. "Why the devil came you between us? I was hurt beneath your arm!"

"I thought all for the best," whispered Romeo.

"A plague on both your houses! They have made worms' meat of me." Then Mercutio let go his last breath.

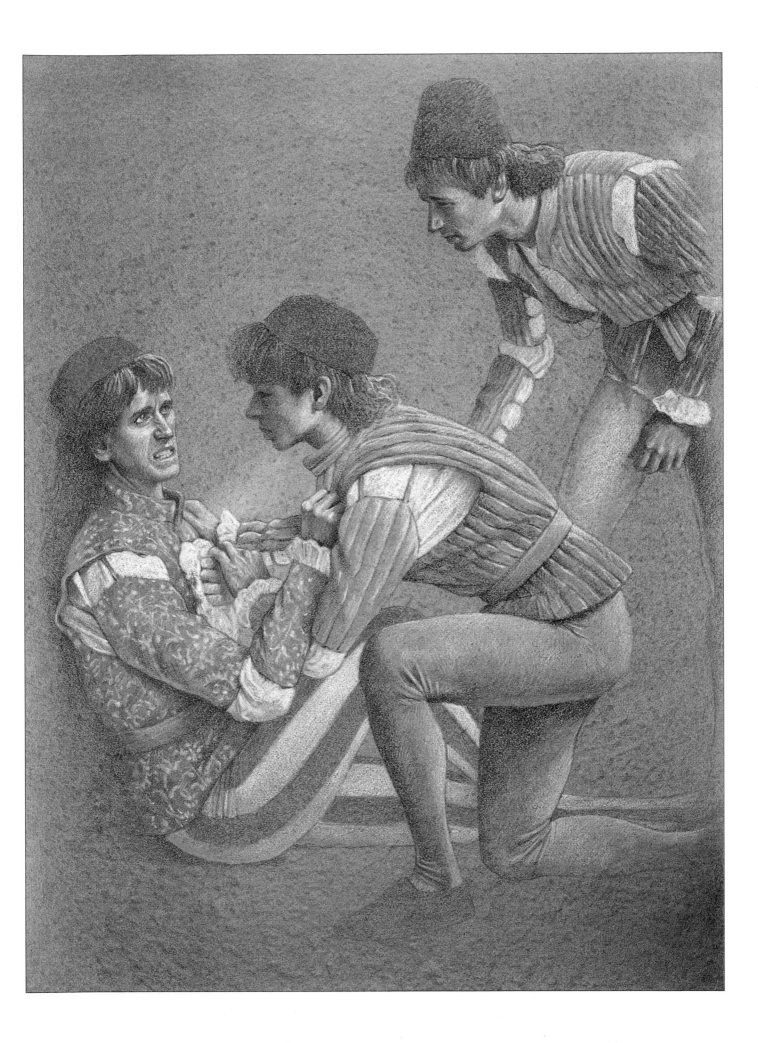

Wild with rage, Romeo leaped to his feet. "Now, Tybalt, take back the 'villain' that late you gave me. Mercutio's soul is but a little way above our heads. Either thou, or I, must go with him."

Tybalt was on him in a flash. But Romeo fought like a mad dog. When the battle was over, Tybalt lay dead on the pavement.

"Romeo, away, be gone!" cried Benvolio. "The prince will doom thee death! Go. *Go!*"

A crowd was already gathering as Romeo fled. When Prince Escalus arrived and saw the day's bloody work, he was furious. "Who began this fray?" he demanded.

Honest Benvolio told all, exactly as it had happened.

"He lies!" shrieked Lady Capulet. "I beg for justice, Prince. Romeo slew Tybalt. Romeo must not live."

The prince pronounced his judgment: "Romeo slew Tybalt, Tybalt slew Mercutio. For this I banish Romeo. If he is found in Verona, that hour is his last."

Juliet was in her chamber, eager for night to fall so that her young husband could come to her side. Her joy was shattered when the nurse arrived, wringing her hands. "He's dead!" she moaned. "He's dead!"

Juliet's heart went cold. "Romeo dead?" she cried.

"No, no, Tybalt is dead, killed by Romeo, who is banished for the crime."

Juliet staggered back. "O serpent heart! O angel-faced fiend! Romeo, how opposite you are to what you seem."

"There's no trust, no faith, no honesty in men," wept the nurse. "Shame come to Romeo!"

The words stung Juliet, and brought her love for Romeo to the fore. "Blistered be thy tongue, Nurse. Romeo was not born to shame. Nor to be... Oh, Nurse! Did you say Romeo was banished?" She sank to her knees. "Banished. My Romeo banished."

Then her tears fell like a summer shower indeed.

Romeo had fled to Friar Lawrence, and there learned of the prince's sentence. "Banished?" he wailed. "Be merciful, say 'death'. Exile holds more terror."

"Rude unthankfulness!" the friar scolded. "The law calls for death. This banishment is dear mercy."

"'Tis torture, and not mercy. Heaven is here, where Juliet lives. Outside Verona's walls is no world, only torture, purgatory, hell itself." He flung himself to the floor, wracked with grief.

"Arise!" said Friar Lawrence urgently. "Someone is here!"

It was the nurse, with word of Juliet. "She is much like him. Blubbering and weeping, weeping and blubbering. Stand up and you be a man. Stand up, for Juliet's sake."

"Your wife awaits," said Friar Lawrence. "Fly to her side. Spend there your wedding night, then flee to Mantua before the break of day. I will work ceaselessly to set things right. If all goes well, we will bring you home ere long."

Friar Lawrence was not the only one planning to send a husband to Juliet. Her father met with Count Paris that very night. "I apologize, sir," said Lord Capulet to the count. "But things have fallen out so unluckily that we have had no time to move our daughter to your suit."

"These times of woe afford no time to woo," replied Paris glumly. "But do commend me to your daughter."

As the count started to leave, Lord Capulet called him back. "Sir Paris, I will make a desperate tender of my child's love. She will be ruled in this by me."

And so Lord Capulet set the date for Juliet to marry Paris that very week.

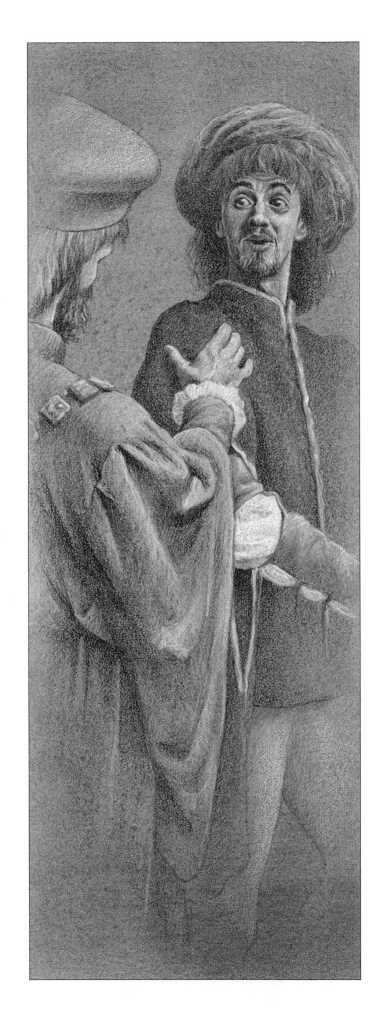

The first rays of the morning sun found Romeo and Juliet side by side. "Will you be gone so soon?" whispered Juliet when Romeo stirred. "It was the nightingale you heard, and not the lark."

"It was the lark, the herald of the morn," replied Romeo sadly. "Night's candles are burnt out. I must be gone and live, or stay and die." He kissed his new wife gently.

"Shall we ever meet again?" she murmured.

"I doubt it not," vowed Romeo. Then he was over the balcony, and on his way to Mantua.

Later that morning Lady Capulet called on her daughter. "I have good news, to wash away the sorrow of Tybalt's death. In but a few days Count Paris shall make thee a joyful bride."

"He shall not!" said Juliet fiercely.

Lady Capulet was startled by her daughter's rebellion. "Here comes your father," she said. "Tell him so yourself."

Juliet threw herself at her father's feet to plead with him. But he was enraged by her refusal of the fine marriage he had arranged. "Hang, beg, starve, die in the streets!" he roared. "Unless you make this match, you are no daughter of mine!"

"O Nurse, Nurse, what shall I do?" sobbed Juliet when they were alone.

"Paris is a goodly man," the nurse said wearily. "And Romeo is as good as dead to you. Please your father and marry the count." The words made it clear that Juliet could no longer confide in her old friend. So she pretended to agree to the marriage.

"Tell my mother I have gone to confess my sins and prepare for the wedding." Then she hurried off to seek Friar Lawrence.

When Friar Lawrence had let her in, she said, "Come weep with me, past hope, past cure, past help."

"O Juliet, I already know thy grief, for Paris has been here. But I can see no way to prevent this wedding."

"Then know this too: You did join this hand to Romeo's. By this same hand I'll end my life, before I wed another."

Friar Lawrence looked with sympathy on the heartsick girl. "Can you be brave?" he finally asked.

"Bid me leap from the battlements of any tower," she replied. "Or lurk where serpents are. Hide me nightly with dead men's rattling bones. Any of these will I do, to live an unstained wife to my sweet Romeo."

"Then go home and consent to marry Paris. But the night before your wedding, drink you of this vial." He handed her a small bottle. "Come daylight, you will be cold and still as if dead, and all will mourn. I, meanwhile, will send word to Romeo, telling him everything. When you wake in your family's tomb, he will be there to take you to Mantua till we can set all to rights."

With trembling hands Juliet tucked the potion in her gown. Then she went home to tell her father she would marry Paris. Lord Capulet was so joyful, he ordered the wedding preparations begun at once.

On the eve of her wedding, Juliet paced her room, staring at the potion. "What if the friar has played me false," she asked herself, "and this be poison, given so that my dying will hide his part in our marriage? No, he is a holy man, and would not do such. But what if the potion works, though not well enough, and I wake too soon? Locked in our family's tomb with long-dead corpses, might I not go mad?"

Evil visions clouded her mind. Yet the thought of marrying Paris was even worse. And so she raised the bottle to her lips. "Romeo, I drink to thee!" she whispered.

❖ ❖ ❖

When the nurse came to wake Juliet for the wedding, she found the girl cold and still. Her cries roused the household, and soon all was weeping and lamentation. Juliet's father was consumed with grief. "All our festival trapping turn to black," he ordered. "All music to melancholy, all hymns to funeral dirges."

In Mantua, Romeo waited eagerly for any word from Friar Lawrence. But no letter had arrived when Romeo's man-servant came galloping in with the news of Juliet's death.

A cold horror stole over the young groom. Trembling, he sent his man to hire fresh horses. Then, when he was alone, he raised his head to the sky and cried, "I defy you, stars! Juliet, I will sleep by thy side tonight."

He made his way to an apothecary shop in Mantua, where he purchased a swift-acting poison. Clutching it as if it were his salvation, Romeo set out for Verona.

❖ ❖ ❖

Later that night Friar Lawrence learned that his letter to Romeo had not been delivered. "If Romeo does not know the plan," he muttered, "there will be no one in the tomb when Juliet awakes." Despite his fear, the old friar determined to go himself, so the girl would not be alone in that awful place.

Moonlight cast eerie shadows over the grave of the Capulets as Count Paris arrived with flowers to lay beside Juliet. At the entrance to the tomb he heard a noise, and slipped into the darkness to hide. When he saw Romeo breaking into the grave, he cried out, "Vile Montague! Can you not leave even the dead in peace?"

"I come with love in my heart," said Romeo. "Do not make me hurt you. Flee now, and say a madman spared your life."

"You will not defile this grave!" roared Paris. He drew his sword, and they fought. But Romeo had the strength of a desperate man, and soon Paris lay dying at his feet. Reaching for Romeo, the count whispered: "Put me beside her."

"You are writ with me in sour misfortune's book," moaned Romeo. He carried Paris into the tomb and gently set down his body. Then he went to Juliet's side.

"O my love, my wife, death that hath suck'd the honey of thy breath hath had no power yet upon thy beauty. I will stay with thee and never from this palace of dim night depart again. Eyes, look your last. Arms, take your last embrace."

He took Juliet in his arms and gave her a final kiss. Then he raised the poison to his lips.

The fatal liquid seized Romeo almost instantly. In but a moment he lay dead at Juliet's side.

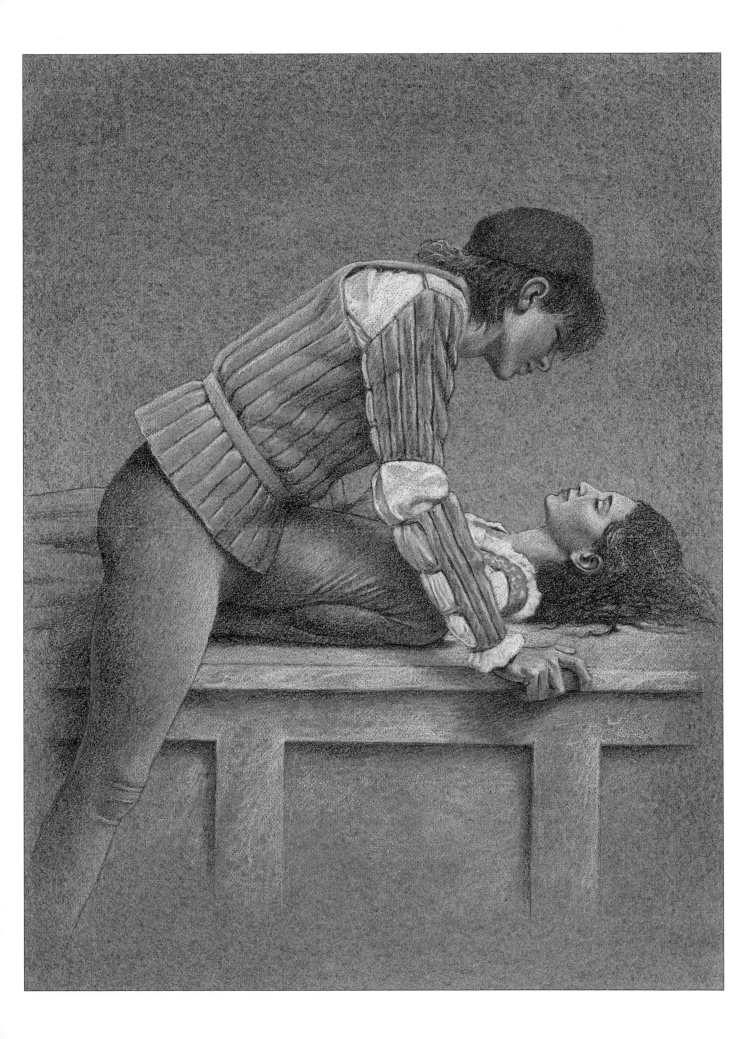

But though Romeo's poison was true, Juliet's was not. She began to stir. When Friar Lawrence arrived, he was aghast to find the bodies of Paris and Romeo.

"O comfortable friar," murmured Juliet, seeing him there. "Where is my Romeo?"

"Come away, my lady," he said softly. "A greater power than we can contradict hath thwarted our intents. Thy husband lies dead, and Count Paris too." Suddenly a shout came from outside. "Quickly!" said the friar. "The watchmen are coming. Flee with me now!"

"Go yourself," Juliet ordered. "I will not."

"I dare no longer stay," Friar Lawrence said, and hurried into the night.

Alone in the tomb, numb with grief, Juliet gazed at Romeo. She saw the bottle of poison in his hand and gently took it. "Churl," she said with sad fondness. "Drunk all, and left no friendly drop to help me follow? I will kiss thy lips, in hope some poison yet doth linger there."

She leaned to kiss him, then drew back in terrible anguish. "Thy lips are still warm!"

From outside came the shouts of watchmen drawing closer.

"A noise?" said Juliet. "Then I'll be brief." Drawing Romeo's dagger, she pressed it to her chest and whispered, "O happy dagger, this is thy sheath. There rust, and let me die." Then she buried the blade in her heart.

A dreadful silence descended on the tomb, broken only when the watchmen arrived and set up a cry throughout Verona.

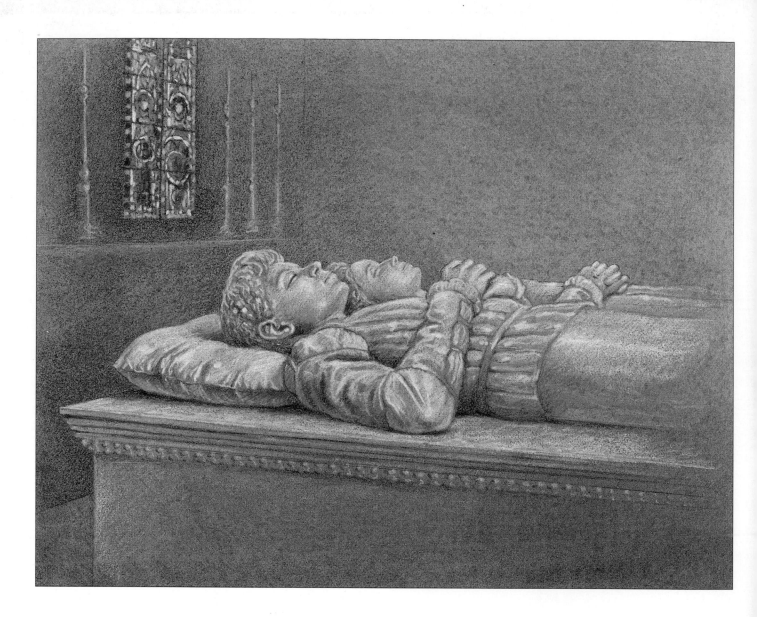

As dawn began to paint the sky, mourners gathered at the tomb of the Capulets. There Friar Lawrence, brought back by the guards, untangled the sad tale for all to hear.

Prince Escalus, caught between rage and sorrow, chided the parents. "See what a scourge is laid upon your hate, that heaven finds means to kill your joys with love."

But with their lives, so needlessly lost to their families' hatreds, the young lovers had at least bought peace. Capulet and Montague, united by grief, pledged an end to the feud. In time they raised statues of Romeo and Juliet, statues of purest gold to mark such a true love, so that the two — tragically parted in life — would be ever remembered together in their death.

❖ ❖ ❖